AISyS 2025

The Second International Conference on AI-based Systems and Services

September 28th - October 2nd, 2025

Lisbon, Portugal

AISyS 2025 Editors

Joseph G Vella, University of Malta, Malta

Printed from e-media with permission by:

Curran Associates, Inc.
57 Morehouse Lane
Red Hook, NY 12571

Some format issues inherent in the e-media version may also appear in this print version.

International Academy, Research, and Industry Association (IARIA)
412 Derby Way
Wilmington, DE 19810

Phone: (408) 893-6407
Fax: (408) 527-6351

petre@iaria.org

Additional copies of this publication are available from:

Curran Associates, Inc.
57 Morehouse Lane
Red Hook, NY 12571 USA
Phone: 845-758-0400
Fax: 845-758-2633
Email: curran@proceedings.com
Web: www.proceedings.com

Table of Contents

AISyS 2025

Forward

The Second International Conference on AI-based Systems and Services (AISyS 2025), held on September 28 – October 1, 2025 in Lisbon, Portugal, continued a series of events covering a broad spectrum of AI focused topics.

AI-based solutions for monitoring, control, decision making are expected to increase the capability of systems providing mechanism for predictions, optimization, risk minimization by interpreting situations and large volumes of data.

A variety of domains (Ambiental, Tactile, Language Processing, Tracking, Healthcare, Ecology, etc.) expanded in the last years based on practical advances provided by Artificial Intelligence (AI). Machine learning AI-based discovery and learning allow deep-learning (and unlearn obsolete knowledge), accurate forecasts, fault prevention and detection, as well as prediction of special diseases. Practical AI-based services in Internet of Things (IoT), Transportation systems, Cyber-systems, Citizen-centric systems, and others reached new levels of usability and quality.

Similar to the previous edition, this event continued to be very competitive in its selection process and very well perceived by the international AI community. As such, it is attracting excellent contributions and active participation from all over the world. We were very pleased to receive a large amount of top quality contributions.

We take here the opportunity to warmly thank all the members of the AISyS 2025 technical program committee as well as the numerous reviewers. The creation of such a broad and high quality conference program would not have been possible without their involvement. We also kindly thank all the authors that dedicated much of their time and efforts to contribute to the AISyS 2025. We truly believe that thanks to all these efforts, the final conference program consists of top quality contributions.

This event could also not have been a reality without the support of many individuals, organizations and sponsors. We also gratefully thank the members of the AISyS 2025 organizing committee for their help in handling the logistics and for their work that is making this professional meeting a success.

We hope the AISyS 2025 was a successful international forum for the exchange of ideas and results between academia and industry and to promote further progress in AI research. We also hope that Lisbon provided a pleasant environment during the conference and everyone saved some time for exploring this beautiful city

AISyS 2025 General Chair

Steve Chan, Decision Engineering Analysis Laboratory, USA

AISyS 2025 Steering Committee

Abdul-Rahman Mawlood-Yunis, Wilfrid Laurier University, Canada
Rahul Agarwal, IBM, USA

AISyS 2025 Publicity Chair

Lorena Parra Boronat, Universidad Politécnica de Madrid, Spain
Sandra Viciano Tudela, Universitat Politecnica de Valencia, Spain
Jose Miguel Jimenez, Universitat Politecnica de Valencia, Spain

AISyS 2025

Committee

AISyS 2025 General Chair

Steve Chan, Decision Engineering Analysis Laboratory, USA

AISyS 2025 Steering Committee

Michael Resch, University of Stuttgart, High Performance Computing Center, Germany
Marc Kurz, University of Applied Sciences Upper Austria, Austria
H.B. Acharya, Rochester Institute of Technology, USA
Ahsan Pervaiz, Google Cloud, USA
Erik Buchmann, Center for Scalable Data Analytics and Artificial Intelligence, Germany
Abdul-Rahman Mawlood-Yunis, Wilfrid Laurier University, Canada
Rahul Agarwal, IBM, USA

AISyS 2025 Publicity Chair

Lorena Parra Boronat, Universidad Politécnica de Madrid, Spain
Sandra Viciano Tudela, Universitat Politecnica de Valencia, Spain
Jose Miguel Jimenez, Universitat Politecnica de Valencia, Spain

AISyS 2025 Technical Program Committee

Manoj Acharya, SRI International, USA
Rahul Agarwal, IBM, USA
Varol Akman, Ihsan Dogramaci Bilkent University, Turkey
Muhammad Atif, University of Florence, Italy
Michael Atighetchi, Raytheon BBN Technologies, USA
Erik Buchmann, Center for Scalable Data Analytics and Artificial Intelligence, Germany
Steve Chan, Decision Engineering Analysis Laboratory, USA
Shuaichen Chang, The Ohio State University / Amazon Web Services, USA
Jinglin Chen, TikTok Inc., USA
Sam Cheng, University of Illinois Urbana-Champaign, USA
Mohammed Dahane, Université de Lorraine, France
Peter Darveau, Digital Research Alliance of Canada, Canada
Charalampos Dimoulas, Aristotle University, Greece
Mounim A. El Yacoubi, Institut Polytechnique de Paris, France
Alain-Jerome Fougeres, ECAM Rennes, France
Yannick Fourastier, Codeurope, Ukraine
Ivan Ganchev, University of Limerick, Ireland / Plovdiv University, Bulgaria
Ilche Georgievski, University of Stuttgart, Germany
Ashish Gupta, BITS Pilani Dubai Campus, UAE

Tzung-Pei Hong, National University of Kaohsiung, Taiwan
Zhipeng Huang, Case Western Reserve University, USA
Ehsan Kazemi, University of Central Florida, USA
Radek Koci, Brno University of Technology, Czech Republic
Marc Kurz, University of Applied Sciences Upper Austria, Austria
Wissam Mallouli, Montimage EURL, France
Danilo Mandic, Imperial College London, UK
Juliette Mattioli, Thales, France
Abdul-Rahman Mawlood-Yunis, Wilfrid Laurier University, Canada
Anabela Moreira Bernardino, Polytechnic Institute of Leiria, Portugal
Eugénia Moreira Bernardino, Polytechnic of Leiria, Portugal
Reza Nourmohammadi, ETS - University of Quebec, Canada
Roy Oberhauser, Aalen University, Germany
Alison Panisson, Federal University of Santa Catarina, Brazil
Ahsan Pervaiz, Google Cloud, USA
Michael Resch, High-Performance Computing Center Stuttgart | University of Stuttgart, Germany
Anirban Roy, Birla Institute of Technology & Science,Pilani, India
Federico Sabbatini, University of Urbino "Carlo Bo", Italy
Addisson Salazar, Universitat Politècnica de València, Spain
Floriano Scioscia, Polytechnic University of Bari, Italy
Carlos M. Travieso-González, University of Las Palmas de Gran Canaria, Spain
Panagiotis Vlamos, Ionian University, Greece
Lei Wang, University of Connecticut, USA
Marcin Wozniak, Silesian University of Technology, Gliwice, Poland
Jing Wu, University of Illinois Urbana Champaign, USA
Jiaxing Zhang, New Jersey Institute of Technology, USA
Tommaso Zoppi, University of Trento, Italy

Copyright Information

The Resilience of the Leisure and Care Economy: Human-Centred Niches in an AI-Driven Labour Market

Ilona Negro
Doctoral Program of Applied Artificial Intelligence
Alma Mater Europea, Maribor, Slovenia
e-mail: ilona.negro@almamater.si

Abstract— **As Artificial Intelligence (AI) is expected to automate up to 30% of current tasks by 2030, it is transforming the structure of work across sectors. Amid this ongoing shift, the Leisure and Care Economy emerges as a sector offering adaptable, future-aligned trajectories. Human-centric professions like wellness instruction, pet care, and craftsmanship represent occupational niches that may benefit from technological advances, building synergies while preserving their essentially human character. This extended abstract proposes the Human-Centric Resilience Model, rooted in Self-Determination Theory and symbolic capital, to examine why these roles endure, evolve, or even grow in symbolic and practical value. The model highlights the distinctive combination of emotional intelligence, physical dexterity, and adaptability as a foundation for this resilience. Drawing on occupational data from O*NET, this paper underscores the economic and social value of these professions. While AI enhances efficiency in routine tasks, multimodal large language models still struggle with complex human interaction. As authentic connections become rarer, such professions may gain premium status. Policy-led training and social revaluation can help build sustainable, fulfilling careers, offering a new perspective on human-AI complementarity in a transforming society.**

Keywords—AI and labour; human-centric work; leisure and care economy; emotional intelligence; automation resilience.

I. INTRODUCTION

Artificial intelligence (AI) is reshaping labour markets, with up to 30 % of current tasks projected to be automated by 2030 [1][2]. While automation redefines many cognitive and routine roles, occupations often labelled low-skilled within the Leisure and Care Economy, such as wellness, pet care, and craftsmanship, appear as adaptable niches because they depend on emotional engagement, fine motor skills, and situational adaptability [3]. As technology frees up more leisure time [2], demand for authentic human interaction rises; yet these professions remain largely overlooked in labour-market debates despite their growing psychological and social importance [4]. This extended abstract introduces the Human-Centric Resilience Model, a conceptual framework that draws on occupational data and sociopsychological theory to understand why certain emotionally and physically embodied professions retain value amid automation. Beyond its conceptual contribution, the model offers a basis for further research, vocational training, and policy development. In Section II, the theoretical underpinnings of the Human-Centric Resilience Model are introduced. Section III explores the role and limitations of AI in complementing these professions. Section IV discusses societal implications, while Section V outlines policy considerations. Section VI concludes with reflections and directions for future research.

II. HUMAN-CENTRIC RESILIENCE MODEL

The Human-Centric Resilience Model draws on Self-Determination Theory (SDT) [5] and Bourdieu's concept of symbolic capital [6] to identify key attributes that help certain professions resist automation: emotional intelligence, physical dexterity, and adaptability in dynamic environments. In contrast to task-based automation models [1], this framework highlights the psychological and symbolic dimensions of human work, offering a fresh perspective on labour resilience. According to SDT, roles that support autonomy, competence, and relatedness enhance intrinsic motivation, which in turn improves service quality in emotionally rich professions, such as yoga instruction or pet care. While often pursued out of passion, these roles are frequently perceived as fallback options due to their low social status, an image the model seeks to challenge. Drawing on symbolic capital, it reframes them as socially valuable for their authenticity, suggesting they may gain premium status as genuine human interaction becomes increasingly rare [6].

What distinguishes the model is not the presence of any one attribute, but the interplay of all three: emotional intelligence, dexterity, and adaptability, as seen in roles like pet care, where skilled task execution and authentic client engagement combine to resist automation. The model applies O*NET occupational data to assess these features [7]. However, because O*NET does not fully capture embodied competencies, such as finger dexterity, tactile sensitivity, and improvisational responsiveness, complementary data from national vocational training standards and embodied skill frameworks will also be integrated. The model will thus be further developed and statistically validated as part of ongoing doctoral research. This interdisciplinary approach links social psychology, economics, and AI research, contributing a novel framework for understanding human–AI complementarity.

The Human-Centric Resilience Model intersects with labour segmentation theory, which highlights how economic and symbolic hierarchies can shift across occupational categories, but introduces a symbolic dimension that extends beyond traditional economic dichotomies [8]. While the Leisure and Care Economy has historically occupied a marginal or feminised position within secondary labour markets, its roles may gain revaluation in an AI-driven society. Drawing on Bourdieu's concept of symbolic capital [6], the model suggests that scarcity, authenticity, and embodied skill can elevate the status of professions that resist standardisation and automation. As AI increasingly replaces routine cognitive labour, the relative value of human traits, such as emotional presence, touch, and improvisational responsiveness, may rise, particularly in cultural contexts that value relational depth. According to O*NET projections, many of these professions, including wellness instructors, animal care specialists, personal service providers, and skilled tradespeople in hands-on, client-facing roles, are already classified as "Bright Outlook" occupations, indicating high demand and rapid growth [7]. Thus, this economy represents not only a resilient niche but a potential reordering of what society deems premium and desirable work, extending beyond traditional metrics of formal skills to include trust, authenticity, and human presence, as labour market dynamics already reflect emerging shortages in wellness, care, and craft sectors [2][3][4].

While the model provides a useful framework, its generalisability may be shaped by cultural norms, economic structures, and local labour market conditions. Emotional intelligence, dexterity, and adaptability are not universally measured or valued in the same way, which may influence the resilience of these roles across different contexts. Moreover, the model should not be interpreted as predictive for all professions within the Leisure and Care Economy but rather as a lens to examine occupational patterns that combine human authenticity with embodied skill. Further empirical research is needed to validate and refine the model's applicability across regions and sectors.

III. AI Complementarity and Limitations

AI can support human-centric professions by taking over routine tasks like scheduling or data management, allowing workers to focus on what they do best: building relationships and offering personalised care. In data-heavy roles, for instance, generative AI has been shown to improve task efficiency by 5–9 %, freeing up time for more meaningful human interaction [9]. However, limitations remain. Multimodal large language models still struggle with nuanced social understanding and cannot simulate genuine emotional attunement [10]. Likewise, humanoid robots face ongoing challenges in replicating human dexterity and adaptive behaviour in real-world settings [11]. These technical constraints, paired with concerns about depersonalisation in robotic caregiving [12], reinforce the enduring value of human-led services. While AI is increasingly capable of mimicking empathy and emotional resonance in conversation, challenges remain where these qualities must be coupled with physical dexterity and real-time adaptation in unstructured, socially complex environments. This underlines the continued need for collaborative human-AI systems, particularly in the Leisure and Care Economy.

Recent developments in Human-Computer Interaction (HCI), Human-Robot Interaction (HRI), and socially aware AI further reinforce the relevance of the Human-Centric Resilience Model. Even within professions that exhibit resilience to automation, workers must adapt to evolving tools, workflows, and expectations. Lifelong learning is becoming less about formal credentials and more about sustained engagement with dynamic technologies. Studies on personalised robotic systems and adaptive human-robot learning architectures show that human-centric roles increasingly involve building synergies with technology, not resisting it [13][14][15][16]. At the same time, persistent challenges, such as robotic limitations in unstructured environments or the public's cautious trust in continual-learning (CL) robots, highlight why emotionally attuned, situationally adaptable human work remains indispensable in care and leisure domains. Moreover, recent work on communicating robot learning underscores the importance of explainability and multimodal feedback for co-adaptation, trust-building, and collaborative interaction between humans and machines [17]. These findings support adaptability not only as a shield against obsolescence but as a bridge to meaningful human-AI complementarity.

IV. Societal and Policy Implications

This section considers the societal dynamics and policy factors that can strengthen the positive effects of the Human-Centric Resilience Model, recognising that the patterns it captures are already emerging and can be reinforced under favourable conditions.

A. Societal implications

The Human-Centric Resilience Model highlights emotional intelligence and adaptability as qualities that remain in demand as clients increasingly seek authentic interpersonal experiences, rooted in the psychological need for relatedness [5]. The growing popularity of personalised wellness services has brought new attention to the Leisure and Care Economy, yet these professions still require societal revaluation to reflect their emotional and cognitive significance [4]. Sustained interest in such roles, however, depends on broader factors, including economic stability, technological shifts, and individual attitudes toward AI and robotics, all of which shape client trust in care and leisure services [18][19]. These complex dynamics reinforce the model's relevance while underscoring the need for further research into its cross-sector and cross-cultural applicability.

B. Policy Implications

To unlock the potential of the Leisure and Care Economy, policies should support vocational training that combines emotional intelligence with digital literacy, equipping workers to use AI tools without losing the human dimension of their roles. Public campaigns can help reframe these professions as essential, purpose-driven careers that foster authentic connection and emotional resilience in an increasingly automated and socially fragmented world [5].

V. Conclusion

The Leisure and Care Economy shows unexpected resistance to automation because its work is fundamentally human-centric, rooted in emotional intelligence, dexterity, and on-the-spot adaptability. The Human-Centric Resilience Model offers a new lens on this resilience by foregrounding psychological and symbolic dimensions often missed in task-based forecasts. Although the model is not a panacea for the wider labour-market disruptions brought by AI, it spotlights a specific segment, frequently dismissed as low-skill and low-wage, that merits strategic attention. Revaluing these professions through targeted training and policy support can create sustainable, fulfilling careers and help preserve genuine human connection in an increasingly automated society. Applicability will, however, differ across cultural and economic contexts, underscoring the need for further empirical research. Overall, this work adds a practical, human-centred perspective to ongoing conversations about effective human–AI collaboration. While the model is theoretical, it offers practical insights into workforce development and policy-making in sectors where human presence remains a core value.

Acknowledgement

The author thanks Prof. Matjaž Gams for his insightful guidance and valuable feedback. This research was conducted as part of the course Artificial Intelligence: Future Trends and Demands, and the supportive academic environment is gratefully acknowledged. Any opinions, findings, or conclusions expressed in this paper are those of the author and do not necessarily reflect the views of the affiliated institutions.

References

[1] C. B. Frey and M. A. Osborne, "The future of employment: How susceptible are jobs to computerisation?" Technological Forecasting and Social Change, vol. 114, pp. 254–280, 2017.

[2] McKinsey Global Institute, "The economic potential of generative AI: The next productivity frontier," 2023. [Online]. Available: https://www.mckinsey.com/business-functions/mckinsey-digital/our-insights/the-economic-potential-of-generative-ai-the-next-productivity-frontier. [retrieved: July, 2025].

[3] M.-H. Huang, R. T. Rust, and V. Maksimovic, "The feeling economy: Managing in the next generation of artificial intelligence (AI)," California Management Review, vol. 61, no. 4, pp. 43–65, 2019.

[4] Global Wellness Institute, "Global wellness economy monitor 2024," 2024. [Online]. Available: https://globalwellnessinstitute.org/industry-research/2024-global-wellness-economy-monitor. [retrieved: July, 2025].

[5] R. M. Ryan and E. L. Deci, "Self-determination theory and the facilitation of intrinsic motivation," American Psychologist, vol. 55, no. 1, pp. 68–78, 2000.

[6] P. Bourdieu, Distinction: A Social Critique of the Judgement of Taste. Harvard Univ. Press, 1984.

[7] O*NET Online. "O*NET Resource Center," [Online]. U.S. Department of Labor. Available: https://www.onetonline.org/ and https://www.onetonline.org/find/bright. [retrieved: July, 2025].

[8] M. Reich, D. M. Gordon, and R. C. Edwards, "A theory of labor market segmentation," The American Economic Review, vol. 63, no. 2, pp. 359–365, 1973.

[9] R. Taiwo et al., "Generative AI in the construction industry: A state-of-the-art analysis," *arXiv preprint*, 2024. [Online]. Available: https://doi.org/10.48550/arXiv.2402.09939. [retrieved: July, 2025].

[10] H. Hu et al., "EmoBench-M: Benchmarking emotional intelligence for multimodal large language models," *arXiv preprint*, 2025. [Online]. Available: https://doi.org/10.48550/arXiv.2502.04424. [retrieved: July, 2025].

[11] X. Zhao, "Research on the application of humanoid robots," in Proceedings of the 2nd International Conference on Software Engineering and Machine Learning, vol. 75, 2024, Art. no. 20240507, doi: 10.54254/2755-2721/75/20240507.

[12] R. Jain and S. K. Dixit, "Revolutionising the future: Exploring the multifaceted advances of robotic technologies," Adv Rob Tec, vol. 1, no. 1, 2023. doi: 10.23880/art-16000101.

[13] B. Irfan, A. Ramachandran, S. Spaulding, S. Kalkan, G. I. Parisi, and H. Gunes, "Lifelong learning and personalisation in long-term human–robot interaction (LEAP-HRI)," in *Proc. 17th ACM/IEEE Int. Conf. on Human–Robot Interaction (HRI)*, 2022, pp. 1261–1264. [Online]. Available: https://api.semanticscholar.org/CorpusID:232136609. [retrieved: July, 2025].

[14] C. E. Clabaugh and M. J. Matarić, "Robots for the people, by the people: Personalising human–machine interaction," Science Robotics, vol. 3, 2018. [Online]. Available: https://api.semanticscholar.org/CorpusID:52074708. [retrieved: July, 2025].

[15] A. Ayub, C. L. Nehaniv, and K. Dautenhahn, "Interactive continual learning architecture for long-term personalisation of home service robots," in *Proc. IEEE Int. Conf. on Robotics and Automation (ICRA)*, 2024, pp. 11289–11296. [Online]. Available: https://doi.org/10.1109/ICRA57147.2024.10611386. [retrieved: July, 2025].

[16] A. Ayub et al., "A human-centered view of continual learning: Understanding interactions, teaching patterns, and perceptions of human users toward a continual learning robot in repeated interactions," *ACM Trans. Hum.–Robot Interact.*, 2024. [Online]. Available: https://doi.org/10.1145/3659110. [retrieved: July, 2025].

[17] S. Habibian, A. A. Valdivia, L. H. Blumenschein, and D. P. Losey, "A review of communicating robot learning during human–robot interaction," *arXiv preprint*, vol. abs/2312.00948, 2023. [Online]. Available: https://api.semanticscholar.org/CorpusID:265609440. [retrieved: July, 2025].

[18] J. Bergdahl, R. Latikka, M. Celuch, I. Savolainen, E. Mantere, N. Savela, and A. Oksanen, "Self-determination and attitudes toward artificial intelligence: Cross-national and longitudinal perspectives," Telematics and Informatics, vol. 82, p. 102013, 2023, doi: 10.1016/j.tele.2023.102013.

[19] V. Yoganathan, V.-S. Osburg, A. F. Colladon, V. Charles, and W. Toporowski, "Societal Attitudes Toward Service Robots: Adore, Abhor, Ignore, or Unsure?," Journal of Service Research, vol. 28, pp. 93–111, 2024, doi: 10.1177/10946705241270736.

The Disruptiveness of Artificial Intelligence in Higher Education: A Focus on Academic Roles, Tasks, and Creative Autonomy

Francis Guambe
Department of Information Systems, North-West University, South Africa

Phemelo Meleloe
Department of Information Systems, North-West University, South Africa

Mdoko Ayanda
Department of Information Systems, North-West University, South Africa

Nkosinathi Mndawe
Department of Information Systems, North-West University, South Africa

Sternan Van Niekerk
Department of Information Systems, North-West University, South Africa

Joshua Ebere Chukwuere
Department of Information Systems, Technology Enhanced Learning and Innovative Education and Training in South Africa (TELIT-SA), North-West University, South Africa
Joshchukwuere@gmail.com

Yakub Kayode Saheed
Department of Information Systems, North-West University, South Africa
kayodesaheed@gmail.com

***Abstract*— The speedy introduction of Artificial Intelligence (AI) into higher education is creating transformative efficiencies and disrupting existing academic positions and creative professional practices. This research explores the vicarious impacts of AI as an enabler and a disruptor and its ramifications for academic work and intellectual creativity using rapid literature review (RLR). The study contributes to the ongoing debate on the disruptive nature of AI on academic jobs through an analysis of the impacts on academic roles and tasks and creative autonomy. By interrogating the disruptive potentials of AI, the researchers call upon institutional leaders to balance the inclusion of technology with the retention of intellectual diversity and employment sustainability while ensuring innovation is being done in line with the mission of higher education. By comparison, the research found that the disruptiveness of AI in academic job roles, tasks, and creativity is not resulting in job losses but instead is creating innovative new job roles. Equally important, the research unpacks the notion that any disruptiveness of AI can be mitigated in spite of the known climate of ethical considerations, with assumptions of a more considered approach and engaged strategies. In the future, academics and scholars should continue to locate and investigate ways to better integrate AI into the academic job ecosystem while maintaining the provenance of existing employment.**

Keywords-Academic employment, Academic labor, Artificial intelligence, Creativity, Disruptiveness, Higher education, Intellectual creativity.

I. Introduction

The integration of Artificial Intelligence (AI) into higher education has become an influential transformation for pedagogical practice, administrative workflows, and research practice. While AI-powered tools, such as adaptive learning platforms, auto-grading, and predictive analytics, provided potential for increased efficiencies and education individualization [1]. The speed of their introduction into higher education has driven discussion around the disruptive implications of academic employment and creative intellectual labour. This interplay of AI as both a facilitator and a disruptor is the focal point of this research, which explores how AI reshapes academic roles, tasks, and intellectual autonomy in the academy. The question would be, how is the integration of AI in higher education disrupting academic roles, tasks, and creative autonomy?

The displacement of conventional academic roles is cause for concern. Research suggests that, by automating administrative and instructional activities (for example, student advising, content facilitation), AI is in danger of displacing non-specialized faculty roles and creating opportunities for faculty with AI literacies [2]. For example, chatbots, such as Georgia Tech's Jill Watson, successfully reduce administrative load, but it rests on the question of whether that load is worth the loss of human mentorship [3]. In regard to creative processes like generating research topics, research objectives and questions, hypotheses, designing curricula, or co-authoring academic papers, AI's role calls into question conventional definitions of intellectual originality in Higher Education Institutions (HEIs). At the same time, instruments like Generative Pre-trained Transformer 4 (GPT-4) are redefining HEI's academic and non-academic processes. GPT-4 has opened the door for the democratization of ideation, critics contend, and it opens the door for a homogenization of scholarly creativity and risk, displacing critical thought altogether [4]. Although GPT-4 is the recent form of GPT, which is part of deep learning developed by OpenAI for natural language processing and generating text.

While existing literature often segments its analysis of AI's impact into either employment trends or pedagogical innovation, with little exploration of both, with a specific analysis of academic roles, tasks, and creativity. This study bridges that gap by interrogating how AI reshapes both the labor dynamics and creative ecosystems of academia in higher education. Drawing on frameworks from constructivist learning theory [5] and critical posthumanism [6], the analysis reveals tensions between efficiency-driven AI adoption and the humanistic values of academia. For example, while AI can amplify productivity in academic research through tools like semantic analysis software [7], its algorithmic determinism may constrain unconventional, interdisciplinary inquiry [8]. Similarly, while adaptive learning platforms cater to diverse student needs, their reliance on data-driven profiling risks reducing lecturers (educators) to "curators" of pre-packaged content, undermining pedagogical creativity [9].

Furthermore, this research is aimed at opposing the notion that the use of AI technologies in higher education will make teaching redundant or will stifle creativity within academics. More precisely, the research intends to:

- Provide rational evidence that asserts that AI will promote creativity in research as well as in personalized learning.
- Convince those in the teaching profession to embrace change; that is, how AI technologies do not interfere with many routine tasks but rather extend and facilitate the teaching vocation.
- Tackle ethical issues, including but not limited to transparency and bias, and yet advocate for the use of AI as an enhancer of academia.
- Show examples of how AI promotes growth and brings people together to create a more active engagement of the academic community.

The whole article was structured in the following manner: Methodology; Brief on the role of Artificial Intelligence (AI) in higher education; Limitations and challenges of AI in academia; Enhance the use of AI in the academic process; AI in academic job transformation; Empirical evidence against job loss; Ethical considerations in ai integration in higher education; Conclusion, and References.

II. Methodology

Academic research can be conducted using primary and secondary data, as well as literature review, such as systematic literature review, narrative review, rapid review, scoping review, and many others. However, the research questions and resources available can determine whether rapid review, narrative review, and systematic literature review can be used [68].

A. Search strategy

This study adopted a rapid literature review (RLR), which is commonly used as a rapid review. According to Smela et al. [69], rapid review is an alternative to systematic literature review, which helps speed up the analysis of existing published research. This method is applied in carrying out social, business, and other research, including information systems (IS) research. However, using RLR in IS research can be done in different ways involving some level of process, but not a systematic process. The process of applying RLR begins with drafting or brainstorming out a research topic and discovering relevant academic papers within the research scope [70].

Some researchers advise applying a systematic method in RLR involving pulling, summarizing, and interpreting existing literature [70][71]. According to Levy and Ellis [71], this process involves input (gathering and screening literature) and outputs (interpreting and reviewing writing). This ensures that quality is maintained while in-depth research is done to increase available literature [72]. Through RLR in the study, the researchers formulated the research ideas, topic, collected relevant literature, and analyzed it in writing a comprehensive review. Keywords like "impact of AI in academic jobs", "AI", "AI in academic", "AI in education", "AI and fear of job", "AI ethical considerations", and many more related keywords were used in the study. The used literature was searched from academic databases like Scopus, ResearchGate, Web of Science (WoS), IEEE Xplore, ERIC, and ScienceDirect, as well as grey literature sources like Google Scholar and Conference proceedings. The search began with screening through potential research topics, analyzing the abstract, and scrutinizing the content of a given paper (article) found within the research title.

Based on the main research objectives, the following research questions guided the study, which can be converted to research objectives:

1. What are the roles of AI disruption in HE?
2. What are the limitations and challenges of AI disruptions in academia?
3. How is AI enhancing the academic process?
4. How is AI transforming academic jobs?
5. In what ways can the fears of job loss through AI disruption be addressed?
6. What ethical considerations impact the integration of AI in HE?

B. The search scope

As RLR was deployed in the study, the inclusion/exclusion criteria were defined within a timeframe involving a number of academic studies, which assisted in answering the research questions as well as addressing the core research objective. This was done to address the question of credibility associated with the literature review (RLR). Also, a rigorous process was deployed to validate the applied RLR in the study in making the findings reliable and usable for decision-making.

Inclusion/exclusion criteria: The study included only documents written in English, sourced from academic databases and grey literature. Also, only peer-reviewed materials were used and published within the stated timeframe as indicated below. While the exclusions were documents written in languages other not English, non-peer-reviewed materials, as well as materials (documents) outside the scope of the article.

Timeframe: This article sourced peer-reviewed materials within the research scope and published between 2021 – 2024. A total of 36 materials were considered appropriate in addressing the research objectives, while additional published papers outside the timeframe were used to enrich the quality of the article.

III. Brief on the Role of Artificial Intelligence (AI) in Higher Education

AI continues to transform higher education institutions in developed and developing nations. This section of the paper highlights the comprehensive roles of AI in higher education.

A. *Definition of AI in a higher education context*

AI refers to the capability of a computer system to perform functions normally associated with human intelligence, such as perception, understanding of language, learning, reasoning, solving problems, and so forth [10]. In higher education, AI helps to enhance the various administrative roles and tasks, and academic processes. Some of the primary applications include:

- *AI-assisted grading:* AI systems can accurately assess the students' assignments and examinations. Consequently, it enables the academics (instructors) to give feedback in good time, thus reducing the workload for the academics (instructors) [11].
- *AI content development:* Some AI technologies can assist in the development and organization of educational materials, ensuring that the materials are up to date and appropriate for particular learning outcomes [12].
- *Virtual tutors:* Such AI-led teachings allow individual students to receive proper instruction depending on their measurements and promote active engagement even beyond formal classroom activities [13].
- *Administrative AI systems:* Incorporation of AI in such systems enhances organizational productivity by automating functions that include, but are not limited to, scheduling, allocation of various resources, and managing student enrollments [14].

B. *Benefits of AI integration and current applications in higher education*

AI contributes significantly to enhancing the effectiveness of administrative activities in post-secondary institutions. The automated systems can carry out processes like scheduling, financial aid allocation, and enrolment management with minimal human intervention, thus reducing operational costs and errors [15]. Thanks to improved efficiency, the administrative staff can focus on other strategic goals, hence promoting an organization that is less rigid and more flexible.

In other words, the goal of AI is to provide individualized learning by using big data gathered through students' performance evaluation and recommending appropriate resources and learning paths [16]. This personalization enhances learners' motivation towards their studies and improves academic performance [17]. Besides, such insights driven by AI technology help lecturers diagnose issues and act on them in advance, thereby improving the learning process.

The implementation of AI in higher education has also presented itself through numerous methods in administrative roles and tasks, as well as instructional improvements. For example, AI adaptive learning platforms are used, where the content type and level of difficulty change according to the student's performance [18]. Also, it presents:

- *Chatbots for student enquiries:* Their work is complemented by AI-based chatbots, which can immediately respond to frequent queries from students on issues of admission, courses, and other support services, thereby relieving the human resources of such services for more complex issues [19].
- *Programs that check for and deter plagiarism:* For instance, Turnitin and other programs that analyze a student's work for similarities use natural language processing (NLP) and other measures to ensure that students do not engage in academic dishonesty practices [20].
- *Advanced analytics:* AI can help identify students who are at risk of withdrawing, predict outcome performance, and recommend corrective measures to improve successful completion and retention rates by applying student data as an additional layer [21].

IV. Limitations and Challenges of AI in Academia

The role of AI in academia continues to be confronted with some limitations and challenges. This section of the study provides a number of limitations and challenges confronting academics in adopting AI, as identified in the literature.

Technological barriers: There are many positive insights into AI applications in higher education, but some technical problems need to be solved. One of these problems is algorithmic bias, which can be defined as an unintended outcome where an AI system discriminates against individuals based on the lines of the data that it was trained or programmed upon. Additionally, AI is less effective in complex or vague environments simply because it does not possess common sense or the subtlety of human on-the-ground educationists [22].

Social ethical issues: There are pressing ethical dilemmas posed by the implementation of AI in learning institutions, which include but are not limited to the privacy of information. In particular, there is a risk of compromising students' privacy, given that it is impossible to train high-performance AI systems without collecting large amounts of information about people, even students who are under strict protection [23]. Also, considerations on the use of AI in such scenarios should ensure that there is respect for both principles of accountability and transparency to protect students from oppression [24].

AI's limitations in human judgment: While AI offers data-driven insights, automates admin and repetitive tasks, and provides valuable support, it is important to safeguard human judgment and intuition. AI lacks contextual understanding and nuanced decision-making that are often required in teaching [25]. For example, understanding the student's background, emotional state, or unique challenges is something that requires human judgment. Human judgment is influenced by a variety of factors such as experience, intuition, empathy, values, and context. These attributes enable humans to make nuanced decisions that consider diverse perspectives and considerations [26].

V. Enhance the Use of AI in the Academic Process

This section provides enhanced application of AI in academic processes.

A. *AI as a tool for enhancing academic creativity*

The increasing adoption of AI technologies in the higher education sector has led to discussions on such technologies' effects on the teaching profession and levels of creativity in academic environments. Opponents claim that such services are looking to eliminate lecturing and that it is damaging to the human psyche. Nonetheless, this research is in contradiction, claiming that AI should be seen as an ally for lecturers, and not as a rival. It facilitates creativity by automating repetitive and administrative research elements and creating an environment for advanced learning and designing, freeing the academic to concentrate on higher responsibilities, such as mentorship of students. This research looks into the interface between AI and academics with a focus on how innovation can be enhanced in the sector.

In our current reality, the threat posed by emerging technologies, AI included, to creativity, employment, or innovation holds great indications of the advancement of civilization and technological advancement. Nonetheless, if implemented correctly within higher education contexts, AI is capable of improving the academic advancement and creativity of lecturers rather than hindering it. The use of AI in the field of higher education opens up some advantages, including the enhancement of research, inventing new ways of teaching, and even student and teacher interactions. This part of the paper will also prove our position that academic creativity is not abolished by AI; it is simply facilitated by it in many ways.

B. *AI in research*

Integration of AI into research and content generation is probably the most important advancement in furthering academic creativity and productivity. AI-based reading, annotations, and note-taking applications, for example, facilitate the use of research tools in the knowledge acquisition process by automating some aspects. These tools may allow the user to glimpse text from a particular source and highlight only the relevant portions, thus helping to decide if the source is worth going through. This can help academics quickly scan through research papers to pick out the relevant material, deciding which sections need thorough reading and which ones to collect notes on [27, 28].

In addition, AI-developed experimental design software takes advantage of machine learning strategies to improve the variables. Furthermore, it is also expected that the time-intensive and laborious steps to do these studies are automated; therefore, it can free up time to focus on data interpretation and analysis. AI development solutions can also reduce the costs of labor involved in R&D and mitigate the level of human errors. To properly use AI applications to help create experimental design models, researchers must develop models that contain a lot of information and a number of parameters. After implementing these parameters, researchers can produce designs for the research studies that promote increased efficiency [29].

Another practical use of AI in research is utilizing AI-supported tools to assist researchers in writing articles or journals, such as paraphrasing or improving their English language structure. One example is using ChatGPT by entering a prompt to either paraphrase or enhance the language and grammar of your sentence and receiving the output in under a minute. This helps reduce time but also maintains the level of precision and fluidity of the English language in which researchers write their articles or journals. This is very helpful, and finding creative and time-saving AI-related tools will greatly help the research community in those countries that do not have English as their primary language [29].

C. *Enhancing pedagogical methods*

In higher education, we are not suggesting AI will or can replace the human aspects in which lecturers operate; it is simply another tool that they can use to develop creative and personalized learning. Lecturers may use AI-based intelligent adaptive learning systems that examine and diagnose the data of students, such as their performance, individual weaknesses and strengths, and speeds of learning. With this information, the system can offer a personalized experience for each learner, with practices, resources, and content, specifically related to that learner's inquiry path [30]. This would provide different strategies of learning, hence making it easier for the students to grasp what is being taught.

In addition, the administrative load carried by lecturers can be considerably lessened with the help of AI assistants, as certain duties such as grading, tracking attendance, and report writing can be performed without human intervention.

These tools employ natural language processing, optical character recognition, and machine learning, for example, to evaluate and interpret the works and statistics of the students effortlessly. Such innovations assist in alleviating the stress levels on lecturers and also enable an assessment and progression of a student in a considerably quicker period. In India, advanced educational technologies such as ConveGenius are being embraced to promote learning and facilitate administrative work, thus increasing educational effectiveness [31]. Also, smart paper promotes enhanced learning and admin roles and tasks.

D. *AI as a creativity booster*

The creative capacity of AI shall be considered as an enhancement. It is the generation of new concepts and ideas that helps overcome the existing paradigms of thinking. An AI system can help find inspiration and explore imagination in creative ways that are otherwise difficult. AI provokes a broader range of thinking where standard limits and beliefs do not apply. AI is a thinking tool and helps a great deal in fostering creative output by introducing information that is not readily available, such as data, trends, relationships, and even blobs of imagination. This is the reason that creativity is considered a helpful application with two tiers. First, the person will try to come up with solutions that are new and not obvious, the AI creative implementation phrased as there are no boundaries as to how imagination can work, smashing any previous harmful structures of thinking [32]. AI can assist in the creative process together with human beings by developing new areas of research, defining existing and emerging patterns, or even producing creative content such as reports, multimedia teaching aids, and visual sense [33]. AI can share new perspectives or strategies in joint academic activities that will save a great deal of time, even if an individual scholar is looking for such approaches.

VI. AI IN ACADEMIC JOB TRANSFORMATION

The argument that AI will replace human jobs is gaining attention, but some believe that technology will not replace academic or human expertise. AI offers numerous tools and techniques that support and enhance the student learning process. It is not designed to replace lecturers; rather, it serves as a tool that complements human expertise in higher education by automating administrative tasks, providing personalized learning opportunities, and offering data-driven insight [34]. However, it is incapable of critical elements such as human judgment, emotional intelligence, or mentorship and guidance that lecturers bring to the learning experience.

A. *Admin and task automation*

AI technologies have proven valuable in automating several administrative and lecturing tasks, thereby reducing the burden on educators and enabling them to focus on more complex aspects of lecturing. One key area where AI is making an impact is grading and assessment. By using machine learning algorithms, AI-powered grading tools like Gradescope can help lecturers in grading students' work, such as multiple-choice questions, quizzes, and even assignments. These tools streamline the grading process, allowing lecturers to "review and adjust the grades before releasing them to students." [35]. This not only transforms and improves productivity but also enhances the efficiency of feedback delivery, helping students receive timely responses and educators focus on more complex assessments.

AI platforms can support lecturers beyond grading, such as scheduling and administrative aspects of learning. AI can be looked at as a way to support scheduling for daily lectures in the classroom, meeting times, attendance tracking, and student enrollment and report card processing [36]. AI chatbots such as Pounce, used at Georgia State University, can answer frequently asked student questions. While these processes remove the workload from the administration, they improve access to information and related support [37].

B. *Enhancing educational engagement*

Beyond administrative support, AI also plays a pivotal role in enhancing educational engagement. Personalized learning is one such innovation. AI in education can analyze students' learning performance data in real-time and recommend personalized learning resources that cater to their individual needs based on their learning styles, abilities, and progress [38]. By providing these personalized learning methods, "AI enhances engagement and motivation levels for students to suit learning preferences and requirements.". Moreover, using the data gathered, AI can help lecturers understand their students' progress, strengths, weaknesses, and learning preferences, and help them improve where needed.

AI-powered chatbots also improve communication within the educational community. These tools can assist with answering common student questions [37]. With Chatbots offering a personalized and interactive education for students, this ensures that they receive timely support inside and outside of school hours while allowing lecturers to focus on more complex concerns.

C. *The role of emotional intelligence*

In the teaching and learning process, it is a vital skill for lecturers to not only impart knowledge but also play a role in shaping the emotional and social development of students. While AI can analyse and interpret data, it certainly lacks the emotional intelligence capacity to empathize, understand, and respond to human emotions, which play a crucial role in human interaction and decision-making [39]. Humane educators can provide students motivation, help them build their confidence, and offer encouragement in ways that AI cannot. These forms of support are deeply human and contribute to the holistic development of students, ensuring that they feel understood and valued.
In the teaching

D. *Focus on mentorship/guidance and research collaboration*

AI may be able to provide individuals with content recommendations, develop personalized learning platforms, automate feedback, and perform all its other uses in education [40], but it cannot replace the mentorship and guidance educators have to offer. The mentorship role involves more than just knowledge transfer; it includes fostering critical thinking, creativity, and ethical decision-making, all of which require a human touch. Thus, AI can never hope to kill academic jobs but can serve as a tool for transformation. With AI growing and handling tasks such as grading, scheduling, attendance tracking, and others, lecturers (educators) can now spend more time engaging directly with their students in meaningful ways. Instead of acting primarily as content providers, they can take on the mentorship role, focusing on supporting and guiding students through their personal and academic growth and developing their knowledge and skills. In this mentorship role, educators can offer personalized feedback, help students define their career goals, and navigate challenges unique to each student.

Lecturers will also have the opportunity to engage in research collaborations, as AI has taken over many repetitive academic tasks. By gathering and analyzing large amounts of data from different sources, AI can help lecturers gain deeper insights and understanding from research [41]. This will free up their time to concentrate on developing research projects and exploring new ideas. This transition positions lecturers to become leaders in integrating AI into academic research, fostering cross-disciplinary collaborations, and utilizing AI to solve complex, real-world problems.

VII. EMPIRICAL EVIDENCE AGAINST JOB LOSS

Multiple studies show that AI deployment does not inherently lead to widespread job loss in most sectors, including education. Instead, AI transforms roles and improves efficiency, allowing educators to focus on more meaningful, human-centered aspects of their jobs [51]. However, most research leads to the belief that the influence of AI on job markets is more likely to alter and change existing jobs, rather than completely replace them. It is very likely that by 2030, there will be an increase in the creation of jobs in the healthcare sector, at a rate of about 570,000 new jobs due to AI and automation. Approximately 261,000 additional employment opportunities will be created in the construction sector, while the services sector can expect an upsurge of about 152000 new positions. These job increases result from the advantages introduced by AI, which help improve productivity and encourage the growth of new sectors and services. Furthermore, it is estimated that about seventy percent of jobs in the education sector will change within five years due to the great adoption of AI systems in personalized learning, grading, and student management systems in institutions [51].

On the other hand, certain sectors are still predicted to reduce the number of workers due to the introduction of technology. As such, operations in the retail industry are likely to shed around 334,000 jobs, the administrative and support services may suffer a job loss of 309, 000 while about 231,000 jobs are expected to be lost from the operations of the manufacturing sector by the year 2030 [52]. This indicates a red flag about the importance of reskilling and upskilling programs to help people move into new positions where AI works to complement rather than replace people [53]. Nonetheless, employment displacement is a valid concern, but AI is expected to augment, rather than eliminate, the need for many human workers, such as those in decision-making, problem-solving, or positions that require critical faculties. With wise policies and smart investments, South Africa can implement AI and build a better workforce for the work of the future [54].

However, addressing the fear of job loss continues to matter, but the following can be done to tackle the concerns

A. *Reskilling and upskilling in the age of AI*

Reskilling and upskilling are also a significant part of the workforce development plan in view of changing job roles and industry needs due to AI and automation. This means training lecturers for other skills or undertaking other types of jobs as AI does more routine tasks, such as grading and tracking attendance, and analytics of different kinds of data [42]. This will now free up the lecturers to move into more value-added tasks that require human judgment, such as one-on-one mentorship, research, and curriculum design. Upskilling involves the betterment of existing skills of the lecturers themselves so that they would be able to then use these new AI tools within their teaching practices. This allows lecturers to apply AI in creating more personalized adaptive learning environments, where course material can be adjusted in real time according to the needs of every particular student. As AI starts to play a more and more significant role in education, its role should be emphasized in terms of new skills that people will gain, rather than taking jobs. AI literacy programs, tech integration training, and digital teaching workshops can empower lecturers and academic staff to work alongside AI [43].

B. *AI literacy programs*

Similarly, AI literacy programs will be equipping the lecturer with easy ways of integrating AI into the lecture hall. Most of the programs focus on understanding the essential core technologies that constitute AI, using AI tools for teaching/administrative purposes, and leveraging data-driven insights to elevate educational outcomes [44]. Some key components of AI literacy programs include:

Understanding AI algorithms and data processing: By understanding the AI algorithms and the processes involved in data handling, one can help alleviate the anxiety. For instance, AI does not eliminate the job; instead, it reduces the cumbersome administrative duties plus reinforces teaching through data provision. For instance, supervised, unsupervised, and reinforcement learning are some of the AI algorithms that allow lecturers to offer student-centric learning strategies and analytical techniques to measure performance more accurately.

AI literacy programs emphasize practical understanding of how AI is utilized in data management and processing for better results in the respective fields. This helps them to work in collaboration with AI. For example, the use of AI systems also allows grading and offers learning to students according to their comprehension levels. Such systems allow lecturers to concentrate on areas that require creativity, critical thinking, and mentorship, which are the roles that cannot be performed by AI. While doing so, the fear of job loss can be turned into an empowering narrative about how education professionals will be supported in their role through the introduction of AI. For leadership change to occur, these programs help lecturers understand the tools that deny AI, so they can use them with AI to improve teaching and learning toward a more informed structure of education [45].

Using AI-powered platforms to monitor student progress: AI literacy programs also highlight the use of adaptive learning management systems (LMS) to monitor student progress. These AI-powered instructional tools continually monitor the performance and engagement of students [46]. This, therefore, would have the lecturers build customized learning paths, based on every individual's progress; receive real-time analytics, enabling them to quickly identify areas where students are struggling; and automate administrative tasks such as attendance and grading. This automation reduces the lecturer's workload, allowing them to focus on more creative or interactive teaching methods. For instance, platforms like BridgeOne use AI to tailor learning experiences by adapting content to meet individual student needs, providing real-time feedback and support [47].

Using AI for administrative tasks: Another key point of AI literacy programs is empowering lecturers to use AI Turnitin for grading the students' work more efficiently, so that lecturers can greatly reduce the time they spend on grading tests and concentrate more on the curriculum and student mentoring [48]. AI can also provide instantaneous responses to student assignments, and thus, teachers can rate student assignments quickly and find out the weaknesses and needs for improvement without using traditional methods like a pen and paper test.

AI-driven insights for data-driven teaching: AI literacy allows lecturers to develop the potential to harness AI-driven insights in creating teaching strategies informed by data. With the analysis of long data about student performance, AI tools provide active information to the lecturer for adjusting teaching methodologies to the performance and learning styles of individual students [49]. Additionally, AI analytics could identify trends across different classes or modules, which would be useful for better resource allocations and targeted interventions. These insights also help foster a more inclusive and responsive lecture environment, where teaching methods can be adjusted in real-time to meet students' needs.

The collaborative and data-informed classroom: AI literacy programs support lecturers in making their lecture rooms more collaborative and data-driven. AI does not replace lecturers; it supports them so they can focus on human-centered skills such as creativity, critical thinking, and emotional intelligence. These, therefore, enable lecturers to make interactive learning environments since lecturers are freed from administrative tasks and data-driven teaching methods. AI informs better decisions on lesson planning, student interventions, and assessments. Finally, AI literacy programs prepare lecturers for the future, where technology and expertise will team up in an effort to enhance learning environments [50].

VIII. Ethical considerations in AI integration in HIGHER education

AI in education has the power to completely change both the way students are taught and how lecturers present the study material to them [55]. AI may boost learning outcomes in a multitude of ways, from reduced administrative procedures to tailored or customized learning experiences. To ensure that we have a transparent use of technology, these integrations may raise ethical issues that need further handling. We therefore gain more insight into navigating the ethical environment of artificial intelligence in academia by investigating the above-mentioned areas [56].

A. Transparency in applications using AI

The significance of transparency in the adoption of AI cannot be overstated [57]. Since no one can see how they work, complex algorithms can be despised by lecturers and students, still referred to as 'black boxes' [57]. From assigning grades to suggesting materials and evaluating the interactions of students and teachers, the focus becomes the goal; therefore, understanding how the AI system makes decisions [58]. The concern among stakeholders regarding the claims of precision and objectivity in presenting results may stem from the existence of obscurity in the mechanical foundation of AI utilized in the applications [59].

B. Academia's bias and AI

One more significant ethical issue regarding AI systems is the risk of bias. AI systems learn from prior sources of information, so to speak (datasets or models can be biased too) [60]. Which, in most cases, contains the biases that are present in the current society? AI systems have the capabilities of aggravating the existing inequalities in the educational setting; if such are ethnically and gendered in nature, they may produce negative outcomes for those from minority groups [61].

C. Recognizing and reducing prejudice

To mitigate this issue of bias, educational institutions have no choice but to analyse the data that is used for training AI systems [62]. It is therefore necessary to conduct a bias audit regularly on these applications and the datasets, notwithstanding their use. To ensure better accuracy, transparency, and authenticity of the data produced by these AI systems. By reviewing data patterns and trends and the processes of making decisions, organizations can identify and address risks that contain inbuilt biases [63].

The data cannot be the only thing that is examined; the algorithms have to be looked at, too. It is the responsibility of the educational institutions to make sure that AI systems are developed fairly. This could involve the use of strategies such as algorithmic fairness, which seeks to change the way computers process data to reduce biased outcomes [64]. For instance, lecturers could promote fairness in the design of AI applications to prevent equity gaps instead of perpetuating them.

D. *The significance of AI understanding*

Both lecturers and students should have a clear understanding of the role of AI in the education system. For example, users are expected to appreciate the standards of evaluation incorporated in the AI application that critiques the student's essays [64]. Rather than elicit distrust in the use of AI tools, this realization encourages students to use them and even nurtures confidence. Institutions should, however, explore the possibility of providing a comprehensive guide and training materials aimed at explaining how AI systems function, the data used, as well as why certain algorithms are applied. They can be of great value in contributing to the knowledge enhancement of the audience. Involving the staff and students in the AI-related knowledge-gaining process can help organizations understand the technology and promote active engagement with it. Such an approach, apart from addressing the problem of transparency, equips the user to take advantage of the more sophisticated aspects of AI [65].

E. *Privacy and moral leadership*

Alongside transparency, governance and data security are interrelated issues. There's a growing concern over the ethical utilization of student-based information in educational organizations [66]. It is essential to inform the individuals concerned about the kinds of data that will be collected, the purposes of each type, and the individuals who will have access to them. Appropriate use of data also ensures trust, which enhances the relationship between the institution, the students, and staff, and encourages mutual respect. Educational institutions should develop clear data governance policies that restrict the unethical usage of student data. The policy should be such that the context in which the data will be used comes first, so that the students know their rights concerning the collection and usage of data about them [67]. Moreover, to maintain trust, effective policies must be established to protect sensitive information.

IX. CONCLUSION

With AI being integrated within higher education, it has raised a synthesis of innovation and disruption, positioning academic work and creativity in a new lens with a critical lens. This research has shown that while AI tools can enhance efficiencies within the operational side of educational design, they can also automate the administrative aspects of learning, individualize learning experiences, and expedite research processes. The risks of adopting may destabilize the notion of academic work too easily through the automation of administrative tasks that flatten intellectual creativity.

Results indicate that lecturers view AI not as a replacement for educators but as an impetus for a change to their job roles, with occupations that involve lesser degrees of specialized knowledge and expertise experiencing an increased threat of displacement. This aligns with global anxieties that labor is becoming polarized in the digital world. In this paper, researchers contribute to this conversation in three ways. First, the empirical summary illustrates the dual role of AI as both a disruptor and collaborator in academic labor. Secondly, the ethical implications of creativity mediated by AI and the implications for innovation in algorithm-driven contexts. Thirdly, the researchers advocate for AI integration of higher education to consider and protect human agencies by creating hybrid contexts to develop productive educational innovations that reflect human agency and responsiveness and provide opportunities to innovate at the speed of technological efficiency. By interrogating these areas, the findings stimulate future strategies to enact the potential AI offers while trying to avoid lifelong learning, the degradation of intellectual labour, and the elimination of stable employment for academics in higher education.

The rise of AI necessitates rethinking education's expertise to fit with technology, while not losing the irreplaceable human dimensions, such as empathy, thinking, judgment, and being a critical, reflective person (and educator). Students who currently experience personalized learning spaces may need to consider guardrails under a regime of AI content over-dependence to maintain originality and critical thought. Administrators must consider reaching innovation and sustainability at the same time and provide equitable AI access while lacking the austerity that usually comes with efficiency-related roles at the expense of labour rights. Ultimately, the fate of AI in higher education will depend on how it is made subordinate to a humanistic goal. As demonstrated in this study, the potential of AI can only be realized through the use of deliberate and ethical strategies that aim to consider intellectual diversity, work equity, and the preservation of creativity. In emphasizing humanity and agency amid technological integration, higher education will be able to utilize AI as a partner, rather than as a disruptor, to protect against technological innovation overwhelming or even eclipsing the mission of higher education.

REFERENCES

[1] J. Hanson, "Displaced but not replaced: the impact of e-learning on academic identities in higher education," Teaching in Higher Education, vol. 14, no. 5, pp. 553–564, 2009.

[2] C. Kosnik, L. Menna, and P. Dharamshi, "Displaced academics: Intended and unintended consequences of the changing landscape of teacher education," European Journal of Teacher Education, vol. 45, no. 1, pp. 127–149, 2022.

[3] D. Adamson, G. Dyke, H. Jang, and C. P. Rosé, "Towards an agile approach to adapting dynamic collaboration support to student needs," International Journal of Artificial Intelligence in Education, vol. 24, pp. 92–124, 2014.

[4] R. Luckin, Machine Learning and Human Intelligence. The future of education for the 21st century. UCL institute of education press, 2018.

[5] L. S. Vygotsky, Mind in society: The development of higher psychological processes. Harvard University Press, 1978.

[6] R. Braidotti, Posthuman knowledge. Polity Press Cambridge, 2019.

[7] I. H. Sarker, "AI-based modeling: techniques, applications and research issues towards automation, intelligent and smart systems," SN computer science, vol. 3, no. 2, p. 158, 2022.

[8] K. Crawford, The atlas of AI: Power, politics, and the planetary costs of artificial intelligence. Yale University Press, 2021.

[9] S. Dutta, S. Ranjan, S. Mishra, V. Sharma, P. Hewage, and C. Iwendi, "Enhancing educational adaptability: A review and analysis of AI-driven adaptive learning platforms," in 2024 4th International Conference on Innovative Practices in Technology and Management (ICIPTM), 2024: IEEE, pp. 1–5.

[10] S. J. Russell and P. Norvig, Artificial intelligence: a modern approach. pearson, 2016.

[11] S. F. Ahmad, M. M. Alam, M. K. Rahmat, M. S. Mubarik, and S. I. Hyder, "Academic and administrative role of artificial intelligence in education," Sustainability, vol. 14, no. 3, p. 1101, 2022.

[12] R. Luckin and M. Cukurova, "Designing educational technologies in the age of AI: A learning sciences - driven approach," British Journal of Educational Technology, vol. 50, no. 6, pp. 2824-2838, 2019.

[13] T. Alqahtani et al., "The emergent role of artificial intelligence, natural learning processing, and large language models in higher education and research," Research in social and administrative pharmacy, vol. 19, no. 8, pp. 1236–1242, 2023.

[14] M. Shoaib, N. Sayed, J. Singh, J. Shafi, S. Khan, and F. Ali, "AI student success predictor: Enhancing personalized learning in campus management systems," Computers in Human Behavior, vol. 158, p. 108301, 2024.

[15] M. Bond et al., "A meta systematic review of artificial intelligence in higher education: A call for increased ethics, collaboration, and rigour," International Journal of Educational Technology in Higher Education, vol. 21, no. 1, p. 4, 2024.

[16] O. Tapalova and N. Zhiyenbayeva, "Artificial intelligence in education: AIEd for personalised learning pathways," Electronic Journal of e-Learning, vol. 20, no. 5, pp. 639–653, 2022.

[17] J. F. Pane, B. A. Griffin, D. F. McCaffrey, and R. Karam, "Effectiveness of cognitive tutor algebra I at scale," Educational Evaluation and Policy Analysis, vol. 36, no. 2, pp. 127–144, 2014.

[18] L. Chen, P. Chen, and Z. Lin, "Artificial intelligence in education: A review," IEEE Access, vol. 8, pp. 75264–75278, 2020.

[19] M. Al-Emran, A. A. AlQudah, G. A. Abbasi, M. A. Al-Sharafi, and M. Iranmanesh, "Determinants of using AI-based chatbots for knowledge sharing: evidence from PLS-SEM and fuzzy sets (fsQCA)," IEEE Transactions on Engineering Management, vol. 71, pp. 4985–4999, 2023.

[20] M. Kolhar and A. Alameen, "University learning with anti-plagiarism systems," Accountability in Research, vol. 28, no. 4, pp. 226–246, 2021.

[21] W. Villegas-Ch, J. Govea, and S. Revelo-Tapia, "Improving student retention in institutions of higher education through machine learning: A sustainable approach," Sustainability, vol. 15, no. 19, p. 14512, 2023.

[22] G. Marcus and E. Davis, Rebooting AI: Building artificial intelligence we can trust. Vintage, 2019.

[23] F. Kamalov, D. Santandreu Calonge, and I. Gurrib, "New era of artificial intelligence in education: Towards a sustainable multifaceted revolution," Sustainability, vol. 15, no. 16, p. 12451, 2023.

[24] L. Floridi et al., "AI4People—an ethical framework for a good AI society: opportunities, risks, principles, and recommendations," Minds and Machines, vol. 28, pp. 689–707, 2018.

[25] A. A. Rasheed et al., "AI and Ethics, Academic Integrity and the Future of Quality Assurance in Higher Education," 2025.

[26] K. D. Stephan and G. Klima, "Artificial intelligence and its natural limits," AI & SOCIETY, vol. 36, no. 1, pp. 9–18, 2021.

[27] B. D. Lund, T. Wang, N. R. Mannuru, B. Nie, S. Shimray, and Z. Wang, "ChatGPT and a new academic reality: Artificial Intelligence - written research papers and the ethics of the large language models in scholarly publishing," Journal of the Association for Information Science and Technology, vol. 74, no. 5, pp. 570–581, 2023.

[28] S. Atlas, "ChatGPT for higher education and professional development: A guide to conversational AI," 2023.

[29] N. Y. G. Lai et al., "Advanced automation and robotics for high volume labour-intensive manufacturing," in 2020 International Congress on Human-Computer Interaction, Optimization and Robotic Applications (HORA), 2020: IEEE, pp. 1–9.

[30] J. C. Tseng, H.-C. Chu, G.-J. Hwang, and C.-C. Tsai, "Development of an adaptive learning system with two sources of personalization information," Computers & Education, vol. 51, no. 2, pp. 776–786, 2008.

[31] S. Patra. "AWS with ConveGenius' AI aims to educate over 100 million students across country." https://www.educationtimes.com/article/newsroom/99733707/aws-with-convegenius-ai-aims-to-educate-over-100-million-students-across-country (accessed.

[32] Y. Chang, B.-D. Li, H.-C. Chen, and F.-C. Chiu, "Investigating the synergy of critical thinking and creative thinking in the course of integrated activity in Taiwan," Educational Psychology, vol. 35, no. 3, pp. 341–360, 2015.

[33] G. Amato et al., "AI in the media and creative industries," arXiv preprint arXiv:1905.04175, 2019.

[34] N. Rane, S. Choudhary, and J. Rane, "Education 4.0 and 5.0: Integrating artificial intelligence (AI) for personalized and adaptive learning," ed: Nov, 2023.

[35] I. Gambo, F.-J. Abegunde, O. Gambo, R. O. Ogundokun, A. N. Babatunde, and C.-C. Lee, "GRAD-AI: An automated grading tool for code assessment and feedback in programming course," Education and Information Technologies, vol. 30, no. 7, pp. 9859–9899, 2025.

[36] B. B. C. Onwuagboke, C. Nnajieto, R. Nzeako, and H. Umune, "Lecturers' Awareness of Artificial Intelligence Tools for Teaching and Research in Alvan Ikoku Federal University of Education, Nigeria," African Journal of Humanities and Contemporary Education Research, vol. 17, no. 1, pp. 1–14, 2024.

[37] S. Dimitrieska, "Generative artificial intelligence and advertising," Trends in economics, finance and management journal, vol. 6, no. 1, pp. 23–34, 2024.

[38] D. Gm, R. Goudar, A. A. Kulkarni, V. N. Rathod, and G. S. Hukkeri, "A digital recommendation system for personalized

learning to enhance online education: A review," IEEE Access, vol. 12, pp. 34019–34041, 2024.

[39] A. Shukla, A. Algnihotri, and B. Singh, "Analyzing how AI and emotional intelligence affect Indian IT professional's decision-making," EAI Endorsed Trans. Pervasive Health Technol, vol. 9, 2023.

[40] S. Maghsudi, A. Lan, J. Xu, and M. van Der Schaar, "Personalized education in the artificial intelligence era: what to expect next," IEEE Signal Processing Magazine, vol. 38, no. 3, pp. 37–50, 2021.

[41] O. Zawacki-Richter, V. I. Marín, M. Bond, and F. Gouverneur, "Systematic review of research on artificial intelligence applications in higher education–where are the educators?," International Journal of Educational Technology in Higher Education, vol. 16, no. 1, pp. 1–27, 2019.

[42] L. Li, "Reskilling and upskilling the future-ready workforce for industry 4.0 and beyond," Information Systems Frontiers, vol. 26, no. 5, pp. 1697–1712, 2024.

[43] D. T. K. Ng, J. K. L. Leung, S. K. W. Chu, and M. S. Qiao, "Conceptualizing AI literacy: An exploratory review," Computers and Education: Artificial Intelligence, vol. 2, p. 100041, 2021.

[44] J. Southworth et al., "Developing a model for AI Across the curriculum: Transforming the higher education landscape via innovation in AI literacy," Computers and Education: Artificial Intelligence, vol. 4, p. 100127, 2023.

[45] L. Carvalho, R. Martinez-Maldonado, Y.-S. Tsai, L. Markauskaite, and M. De Laat, "How can we design for learning in an AI world?," Computers and Education: Artificial Intelligence, vol. 3, p. 100053, 2022.

[46] C. Halkiopoulos and E. Gkintoni, "Leveraging AI in e-learning: Personalized learning and adaptive assessment through cognitive neuropsychology—A systematic analysis," Electronics, vol. 13, no. 18, p. 3762, 2024.

[47] C.-w. Shen, T.-h. Luong, J.-t. Ho, and I. Djailani, "Social media marketing of IT service companies: Analysis using a concept-linking mining approach," Industrial Marketing Management, vol. 90, pp. 593–604, 2020.

[48] L. Gustilo, E. Ong, and M. R. Lapinid, "Algorithmically-driven writing and academic integrity: exploring educators' practices, perceptions, and policies in AI era," International Journal for Educational Integrity, vol. 20, no. 1, p. 3, 2024.

[49] K. Allil, "Integrating AI-driven marketing analytics techniques into the classroom: pedagogical strategies for enhancing student engagement and future business success," Journal of Marketing Analytics, vol. 12, no. 2, pp. 142–168, 2024.

[50] D. T. K. Ng, J. K. L. Leung, J. Su, R. C. W. Ng, and S. K. W. Chu, "Teachers' AI digital competencies and twenty-first century skills in the post-pandemic world," Educational technology research and development, vol. 71, no. 1, pp. 137–161, 2023.

[51] J. Howard, "Artificial intelligence: Implications for the future of work," American Journal of Industrial Medicine, vol. 62, no. 11, pp. 917–926, 2019.

[52] L. Novakova, "The impact of technology development on the future of the labour market in the Slovak Republic," Technology in Society, vol. 62, p. 101256, 2020.

[53] R. Nowrozy, "GPTs or Grim Position Threats? The Potential Impacts of Large Language Models on Non-Managerial Jobs and Certifications in Cybersecurity," in Informatics, 2024, vol. 11, no. 3: MDPI, p. 45.

[54] A. Sey and O. Mudongo, "Case studies on AI skills capacity building and AI in workforce development in Africa," Research ICT Africa, 2021.

[55] P. Lameras and S. Arnab, "Power to the teachers: an exploratory review on artificial intelligence in education," Information, vol. 13, no. 1, p. 14, 2021.

[56] I. Roll and R. Wylie, "Evolution and revolution in artificial intelligence in education," International Journal of Artificial Intelligence in Education, vol. 26, pp. 582–599, 2016.

[57] W. J. Von Eschenbach, "Transparency and the black box problem: Why we do not trust AI," Philosophy & Technology, vol. 34, no. 4, pp. 1607–1622, 2021.

[58] H. Khosravi et al., "Explainable artificial intelligence in education," Computers and education: artificial intelligence, vol. 3, p. 100074, 2022.

[59] O. Menis-mastromichalakis, "Explainable Artificial Intelligence: An STS perspective," 2024.

[60] J. Stewart et al., "Attitudes towards artificial intelligence in emergency medicine," Emergency Medicine Australasia, vol. 36, no. 2, pp. 252–265, 2024.

[61] A. Hagerty and I. Rubinov, "Global AI ethics: a review of the social impacts and ethical implications of artificial intelligence," arXiv preprint arXiv:1907.07892, 2019.

[62] A. K. Kar, P. Varsha, and S. Rajan, "Unravelling the impact of generative artificial intelligence (GAI) in industrial applications: A review of scientific and grey literature," Global Journal of Flexible Systems Management, vol. 24, no. 4, pp. 659–689, 2023.

[63] P. Esmaeilzadeh, "Challenges and strategies for wide-scale artificial intelligence (AI) deployment in healthcare practices: A perspective for healthcare organizations," Artificial Intelligence in Medicine, vol. 151, p. 102861, 2024.

[64] J. Burrell, "How the machine 'thinks': Understanding opacity in machine learning algorithms," Big data & society, vol. 3, no. 1, p. 2053951715622512, 2016.

[65] A. N. Khan, M. A. Soomro, and A. H. Pitafi, "AI in the Workplace: Driving Employee Performance Through Enhanced Knowledge Sharing and Work Engagement," International Journal of Human–Computer Interaction, pp. 1–14, 2024.

[66] M. B. Kwapisz, A. Kohli, and P. Rajivan, "Privacy concerns of student data shared with instructors in an online learning management system," in Proceedings of the 2024 CHI Conference on Human Factors in Computing Systems, 2024, pp. 1–16.

[67] F. J. García-Peñalvo, "Avoiding the dark side of digital transformation in teaching. An institutional reference framework for eLearning in higher education," Sustainability, vol. 13, no. 4, p. 2021.

[68] J. Chukwuere, "Exploring literature review methodologies in information systems research: A comparative study," Education & Learning in Developing Nations (ELDN), vol. 1, no. 2, pp. 38–46, 2023.

[69] B. Smela, M. Toumi, K. Świerk, K. Gawlik, E. Clay, and L. Boyer, "Systematic literature reviews over the years," Journal of market access & health policy, vol. 11, no. 1, p. 2244305, 2023.

[70] W. Bandara, S. Miskon, and E. Fielt, "A systematic, tool-supported method for conducting literature reviews in information systems," in ECIS 2011 proceedings [19th European conference on information systems], 2011: AIS Electronic Library (AISeL)/Association for Information Systems, pp. 1–13.

[71] Y. Levy and T. J. Ellis, "A systems approach to conduct an effective literature review in support of information systems research," Informing Science, vol. 9, 2006.

[72] M. Tate, E. Furtmueller, J. Evermann, and W. Bandara, "Introduction to the special issue: The literature review in information systems," Communications of the Association for Information Systems, vol. 37, no. 1, p. 5, 2015.

A Prospective Monotonic/Non-Monotonic Transition Zone Impediment for Concept Model-Centric Artificial Intelligence Systems

Steve Chan
VTIRL, VT/DE-CAIR
Orlando, USA
Email: stevec@de-cair.tech

***Abstract*—The increasing use of Artificial Intelligence (AI) has led to a myriad of Swarm Intelligence (SI) opportunities, wherein collective learning can occur, such as Machine Learning (ML) on ML, as well as collective Multi-Criteria Decision-Making (MCDM). Effective ML on ML tends to involve Knowledge Transfer (KT) via a Domain Knowledge Communication (DKC) channel, wherein successful interpretation of both the knowledge and the inferential processes involved is central. This is particularly important when temporal considerations matter. The conveyance of concepts, similar to the functioning of a Large Concept Model (LCM), exhibits promise, and various benchmarks — to ensure such a successful conveyance — have been scrutinized. However, while various efforts have been expended on the machine-centric side of the AI System (AIS) divide, a certain Achilles heel may reside on the human-centric side of the overarching Socio-Technical System (STS) in the form of non-concept model-centric Likert-derived information. This paper will progress through some machine-centric side experimental forays and then hone in on the Likert-centric repertoire on the other side of the AIS divide. A mitigation construct is proposed, and preliminary explorations exhibit some promise.**

Keywords-*artificial intelligence systems; machine learning; Lower Ambiguity Higher Uncertainty (LAHU); Higher Ambiguity Lower Uncertainty (HALU); isomorphic engine; domain knowledge communication; multi-criteria decision-making; decision quality; decision engineering.*

I. Introduction

The efficacy of certain Real World System (RWS) applications, such as Conversational Artificial Intelligence (AI), is often predicated upon consistency and reliability, and this particular facet can be referred to as Conversational AI (CAI) Robustness (CAIR). The responses/assertions provided by the involved CAI Agent (which should be designed to engage in "human-like conversations" by comprehending user intent, maintaining context, and putting forth pertinent responses) should adhere to the principle of CAIR; in other words, a core tenet of CAIR is that CAI Agent responses, once put forth, should maintain their validity (even amidst new user information provided). However, maintaining coherence and monotonicity is non-trivial, as the involved AIS might discern connections (particularly those that are non-monotonic) within the evolving dataset. In the context of CAIR, non-monotonic aspects can arise as incoming information can re-contextualize and/or contradict matters. Yet, enforcing a strict monotonic paradigm can segue to an unnatural rigidity and/or incorrect/irrelevant responses by the CAI. Accordingly, enhanced insight into the CAI behavior at Monotonic/Non-monotonic Transition Zones (MNTZ) can potentially be quite meaningful for elevating CAIR-related coherence and consistency (with the concomitant validity). Yet, this MNTZ element is often not part of CAI architectures, and the involved Repertoire of Likert-based Information (RLBI) training data and associated approach utilized do not necessarily have the benefit of various mitigation elements applied to them, such as in the form of Best-Worst Scaling (BWS) (which identifies "most preferred" and "least preferred" at the subset level), Q-methodology (which illuminates "opinion typologies"), and the like. Certain Subject Matter Experts (SMEs) in this arena attribute this to the hitherto success and novelty of CAI. However, Subsection A will highlight the potential downfall of reliance upon prior successes as architectural validation.

A. Case study of a system-level Achilles heel

The case study related to the Space Shuttle Columbia has been referred to often in various environs (e.g., academic), which focus upon a "learning culture." According to the National Aeronautics and Space Administration (NASA) commission that reviewed the Space Shuttle Columbia case, certain phenomena had become accepted over time; among these, was the "bipod ramp" (which connected the main external fuel tank to the spaceplane component of the Space Shuttle) thermal insulating foam (which prevented ice from forming when the external fuel tank was replete with liquid hydrogen and oxygen, as ice could damage the Space Shuttle, if shed during launch) that had been been observed falling off, in whole and/or in part, on several prior NASA missions (e.g., pertaining to the Challenger, Atlantis, and Columbia) prior to the Space Shuttle Columbia disintegration on 1 February 2003; ultimately, the cause of the disintegration could be attributed to a piece of thermal insulating foam breaking off from the external fuel tank after liftoff, striking the left wing, and causing a perforation that allowed "super-hot atmospheric gases" to enter the wing when the Space Shuttle Columbia later re-entered the atmosphere. As prior missions had been successful, NASA had grown accustomed to this "foam shedding" phenomena. After the Space Shuttle Columbia disintegration, the post-disaster investigation revealed that numerous NASA missions had indeed experienced thermal insulating foam loss, which had gone undetected. According to the NASA commission reviewing the Columbia case, the incident was at least partially attributed to the fact that "the Shuttle is now an aging system but still developmental in character," and "cultural traits and organizational practices detrimental to safety were allowed to develop, including reliance on past success as a substitute for sound engineering practices" [1].

In many ways, this lesson learned also seems to apply to those CAI architectures not treating the CAIR-related coherence, consistency, and validity issue. Indeed, it also seems to apply as a more generalized potential "foam shedding" aspect of contemporary Artificial Intelligence (AI) Systems (AIS); in particular, this may involve the Knowledge Transfer (KT) from an involved RLBI, which is not necessarily optimally conducive for a Large Concept Model (LCM) or concept model-centric Low Ambiguity High Uncertainty (LAHU)/Higher Ambiguity Lower Uncertainty (HALU) module that relies upon a quasi-isomorphic engine. In fact, preliminary experimentation shows that RLBI tends to aggravate matters in the MNTZ for AIS, as its non-concept model-centric paradigm seems to be problematic by introducing: heightened ambiguity, a less robust estimated parameter class (given the non-concept model-centric nature of RLBI), and a greater propensity for spawning towards the Non-deterministic Polynomial-time Hardness (NP-hard) non-continuous, non-polynomial, and non-monotonic side.

B. Contemporary case of a prospective AIS Achilles heel

The overarching rubric of AIS contains AI Control and Decision Systems (CDS) (AICDS), which in turn have Machine Learning (ML) constituent components. These components might involve, among others, LAHU/HALU components. The LAHU/HALU component has RWS application, as it accommodates the temporal element. By way of explanation, if the LAHU component deems that its repertoire [module] contains sufficient apriori experience (i.e., low ambiguity), then it might allow for an increased tolerance towards uncertainty, and likely, the need for more *Big Data* can be curtailed [2]; conversely, if the HALU component determines that there is insufficient apriori experience (i.e., high ambiguity), then it might necessitate more *Big Data*. In essence, the described paradigm equates to a quasi-isomorphic engine, which is better described as leveraging a quasi-LCM approach that segues to enhanced/nuanced semantic context, given the intrinsic ability to orchestrate multimodal inputs and extrapolate towards the desired notion/abstract concept class. The LAHU/HALU amalgam necessarily involves Multi-Criteria Decision-Making (MCDM). In turn, MCDM is typically comprised of Multi-Objective Decision-Making (MODM) and Multi-Attribute Decision-Making (MADM) modules. MODM usually involves multiple objectives, which are often conflicting, and MADM usually involves a singular objective. The counterpoising of the two is crucial. In turn, each of these can be comprised of Subjective Measures (SM), as well as Objective Measures (OM). Likewise, the counterpoising of these SM/OM is vital; otherwise, a variety of SM-related biases are likely to seep into the construct. The described AIS/AICDS is construed to reside within the realm of Decision Engineering (DE)/Decision-Making (DM), and the aforementioned is reflected in Figure 1. The enclosing purple boxes and font of that color pertain to some of the experimental forays presented herein. The blue boxes and font provide some pertinent ontological terms/concepts.

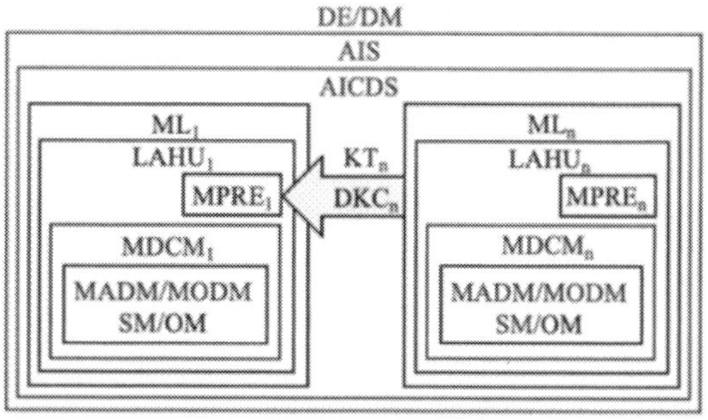

Figure 1. AIS/AICDS ML on ML KT (via DKC) with the LAHU/HALU MCDM (e.g., a MADM/MODM SM/OM counterpoising) supporting a Machine-Processed Repertoire of Experience (MPRE).

The LAHU/HALU's MPRE [module] is, ideally, enriched by KT, via the learnings of other precursor ML(s), such as shown in Figure 1 (e.g., ML_n). The channel by which the KT occurs is referred to as Domain Knowledge Communication (DKC) (e.g., DKC_n in Figure 1). Implicit in the reference to DKC is the prospective ability to convey the specialized knowledge of the involved domain(s); it is thought that a high efficacy approach centers upon the previously referenced notions/abstract concepts/estimated parameter class. Yet, these abstractions often also depend upon their interim notions/Inferred Latent Variables (ILVs), which in turn are, in some form or fashion, somewhat conveyed by various attributes. This paradigm is delineated via a prototypical Latent Variable Model (LVM) (Table I).

TABLE I. SAMPLE LVM CATEGORIES OF ESTIMATED PARAMETER CLASS, INTERIM NOTIONS, AND ATTRIBUTES CATEGORIES

Abstract Concept/ Notion/ Predicted Class/ Unknown Parameter/ Estimated Parameter Class	***Unobserved Variables/ Interim Notions/ Hidden Underlying Factors/ Latent Traits/ Inferred Latent Variables (ILVs)***	***Observed/Observation Variables/ Measured Variables/ Indicators Items/ Measures/ Attributes***

However, when the measured variables and ILVs are not 1-to-1, such as in the case wherein certain attributes are linked to many ILV (1-to-many) and/or many attributes are used to convey the essence of an ILV (many-to-1), then the causal relationships are no longer linear; they are non-linear. In cases such as this, Interpretability and Explainability (I&E) becomes paramount so as to better contextualize the causal pathways. This is non-trivial and the "quantification of joint contributions" is an active research area. Harris, by way of example, suggests joint Shapley values as a measure of joint feature importance within the involved feature sets [3]. Dhamdhere extends this by suggesting the utilization of "Shapley-Owen values" for this type of quantification [4]. Also, while the content related to the KT can indeed be significant, knowledge of the involved inferential process can, in a number of cases, be even more vital, as there may be certain bulwarks established, wherein KT across the DKC does not occur if the I&E threshold is not met.

It can then be ascertained that I&E and DKC for high efficacy ML on ML is a key thematic of this paper. Effective ML upon ML necessitates a certain degree of I&E for operationalizing DKC. I&E is construed to be part of the System Transparency, Explainability, and Accountability (STEA) rubric. In turn, STEA endeavors to mitigate against bias, and while machine-side AIS has been heavily scrutinized, oftentimes, the human-side elements (e.g., individual, institutional bias) "of the larger Socio-Technical System [STS]" have not been treated as robustly [5]. Exemplar biases impacting I&E/DKC include, but are not limited to:

1) Central Tendency Bias

Wang and Liu remind us that RWS data "often exhibit a long-tailed" distribution [6][7]. Within the STS paradigm, human input contributions (towards the repertoire of apriori experience) via modalities, such as Likert-derived information, often tend toward central tendency bias (i.e., a predilection towards the median and away from the min/max), and this is affirmed by Akbari and Sabolic [8][9]. This central tendency bias is likely to obscure/obfuscate the long-tail realities of the involved RWS.

2) Acquiescence Bias

Continuing along the vein of RLBI, Friborg reminds us that these forms "introduce acquiescence bias" [10]. To mitigate against this, it is customary to engage in negation transformations, but the "transformations may introduce errors, as negatives of positive constructs may appear contra-intuitive" (i.e., counter-intuitive) [10].

3) Anchoring Bias

As Yasseri reminds us, Kahneman and Tversky cautioned against the use of certain heuristics, wherein "certain information will be simplified, some ignored, and estimations will be made, thus increasing the likelihood of systematic errors in decisions" [11][12]. This predilection for gravitating towards "immediate examples" in one's mind is often referred to as a "mental shortcut" or "cognitive bias" [11]; an example includes anchoring bias, which involves gravitating towards "the first piece of information encountered" [11]. LAHU/HALU mitigates against this by examining MPRE and making the DE/DM determination on whether more *Big Data* is needed or not to lower the uncertainty.

4) Selection Bias

Of note, Berger reminds us that "the quality of randomization is an under-appreciated facet" and that "improper randomization" can segue to "selection bias" [13]. In essence, the choice of datasets, methods, design, programming, etc. as well as the individuals, groups, etc. selected for analysis (if subject to selection bias) can lead to a failure of "proper randomization" [14]. The significance is that the sample set obtained will no longer be representative of the population set to be scrutinized [15]. Hence, the results will likely be skewed. The LAHU/HALU MCDM can help mitigate against this, as the MCDM well considers the SM/OM counterpoisings for MADM/MODM.

The aforementioned referenced biases, among others, can challenge I&E/DKC and wreak havoc on an AIS/AICDS. To better illuminate this challenge, Figure 2 depicts the Human-Computer Interface (HCI) or Human-Machine Interface (HMI) zone, and the DKC channel is depicted as well.

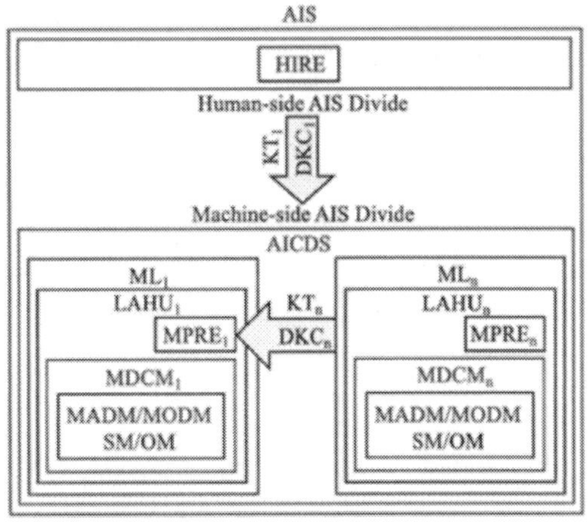

Figure 2. Human-side HIRE and Machine-side MPRE of the AIS Divide with KT/DKCs shown.

In the context of the referenced LAHU/HALU MPRE, the STS Human-Informed Repertoire of Experience (HIRE) side has high potential to skew/bias the STS MPRE side, thereby affecting the entire AIS/AICDS; hence, careful consideration of this issue is needed. *STS elements that can hinder I&E and degrade DKC are deemed to be disruptive for the AIS/AICS, and illuminating some of these STS elements is another key thematic of this paper.* Figure 2 shows that this can come via HIRE, across the KT_1/DKC_1, and affect the involved MPREs, such as $MPRE_1$ (it can also come from $MPRE_n$, across KT_n/DKC_n, and affect $MPRE_1$ in some cases).

Accordingly, this paper delineates the STS HIRE side of an AIS and its potential to adversely impact the STS MPRE side of an AIS. Section I provided an overview, which underscored the import of I&E and DKC for high efficacy

ML on ML, as well as the fact that STS elements, such as HIRE, can potentially hinder I&E and degrade DKC so as to be disruptive for the AIS/AICS.

For the reader's convenience, a listing of acronyms utilized thus far and for the sections that follow is being provided in Table II below.

TABLE II. LISTING OF ACRONYMS UTILIZED

Acronym	*Expanded Form*
AI	Artificial Intelligence
AICDS	Artificial Intelligence Control and Decision Systems
AIS	Artificial Intelligence System
BLUF	Bottom Line Up Front
BWS	Best-Worst Scaling
C	Consistency
CAC	Current Architectural Construct
CAI	Conversational Artificial Intelligence
CAIR	Conversational Artificial Intelligence Robustness
COPRAS	Complex Proportional Assessment
CRITIC	CRiteria Importance through Intercriteria Correlation
D	Hoeffding's D Correlation Coefficient
dCor	Distance Correlation Coefficient
DE	Decision Engineering
DEA	Data Envelopment Analysis
DKC	Domain Knowledge Communication
DM	Decision-Making
ELECTRE	ELimination Et Choix Traduisant la Realité
F	Flexibility
F-VIKOR	Fuzzy VIseKriterijumska Optimizacija I Kompromisno Resenje
GP	Goal Programming
HALU	Higher Ambiguity Lower Uncertainty
HCI	Human-Computer Interface
HIRE	Human-Informed Repertoire of Experience
HMI	Human-Machine Interface
HV	Hypervolume
I	Interpretability
I&E	Interpretability and Explainability
ICC	Information Coefficient of Correlation
IGD	Inverted Generational Distance
ILVs	Inferred Latent Variables
KT	Knowledge Transfer
LAHU	Low Ambiguity High Uncertainty
LCM	Large Concept Model
LVM	Latent Variable Model
MADM	Multi-Attribute Decision-Making
MC	Maximal Correlation
MCDM	Multi-Criteria Decision-Making
MI	Mutual Information
MIC	Maximum Information Coefficient
MINLP	Mixed Integer Non-Linear Programming
ML	Machine Learning
MM	MULTIMOORA
MNTZ	Monotonic/Non-monotonic Transition Zones
MODM	Multi-Objective Decision-Making
MPRE	Machine-Processed Repertoire of Experience
NASA	National Aeronautics and Space Administration
NP-hard	Non-deterministic Polynomial-time Hardness
OM	Objective Measures
P	Performance
PAC	Previous Architectural Construct
PBCC	Percentage Bend Correlation Coefficient
PPMCC	Pearson's [Product]-Moment Correlation Coefficient
PROMETHEE	Preference Ranking Organization Method for Enrichment Evaluation
rho	Spearman's Rho Correlation Coefficient
RLBI	Repertoire of Likert-based Information
RNLBI	Repertoire of Non-Likert-based Information
ROM	Rough Order of Magnitude
ROYG	Red-Orange-Yellow-Green
RWS	Real World System
S	Sensitivity
S/R	Sorting/Ranking
SD	Semantic Differential
SDP	Semi-Definite Programming
SI	Swarm Intelligence
SM	Subjective Measures
SMEs	Subject Matter Experts
STEA	System Transparency, Explainability, and Accountability
STS	Socio-Technical System
tau	Kendall's Tau Correlation Coefficient
TOPSIS	Technique of Order Preference by Similarity to an Ideal Solution
U	Performance under Uncertainty
V	Validity
VC-dim	Vapnik-Chervonenkis dimension
VD	Verification/Discernment
WASPAS	Weighted Aggregated Sum Product Assessment

The remainder of this paper is organized as follows. Section II notes that RLBI potentially worsens conditions in the AIS MNTZ for AIS/AICDS, as its non-concept model-centric paradigm seems to be of some hindrance by introducing heightened ambiguity, a less robust estimated parameter class, and a greater propensity for spawning to the NP-hard, non-continuous, non-polynomial, and non-monotonic side. Section II also notes that Repertoire of Non-Likert-based Information (RNLBI) approaches, such as Semantic Differential (SD), necessitate a higher level of abstraction-level thinking, at the onset, that is more intrinsically akin to the ultimate notion/abstract concept to be expressed. Section III presents theoretical foundations as well as some precursor experimentation, an updated experimental setup (to account for some prospective quantitative speciousness in the literature), and an interim discussion regarding how RNLBI approaches (e.g., SD) — as they are more intrinsically akin to the concept model — will be more amenable for the MPRE via LAHU/HALU processing and may induce less spawning than RLBI. Section IV provides a discussion with some concluding remarks, and some proposed future work closes the paper.

II. BACKGROUND

Despite the criticality of I&E for operationalizing a high efficacy DKC, the treatment of I&E (and its overarching STEA) still remains in a fairly nascent state. By way of example, even the gauging of I&E still tends to be tied to the rudimentary metric of relating I&E to the complexity of the involved AIS/ML architecture. Along this vein, measures, such as "the Vapnik-Chervonenkis dimension (VC-dim)" are often utilized to gauge this complexity [16]. After all, the VC-dim can be emblematic, in a rough sense, of the Rough

Order of Magnitude (ROM) related to the involved number of weights, rules, etc.; indeed, an unwieldy number of, say, rules can readily segue to downstream brittleness issues. Brittleness, which had previously been explored in [17], necessitates a marked change in the paradigm, and I&E can fluctuate accordingly. Generally speaking, the ongoing tectonic shifts do not lend well toward enhancing I&E. Wood asserts that this type of "failure is due to brittle systems" [18]. Druce affirms, and of significance, Druce notes that "this lack of [I&E/]understandability in AIs precludes them from use in critical applications" [19]. Accordingly, this paper centers upon mission-critical RWS AIS/AICDS and revisits various potentially specious notions.

A. Brittleness & Volatility in the MNTZ

The described brittleness and volatility/unpredictability is especially prevalent within the MNTZ, wherein the shift of the involved variables from a monotonic to a non-monotonic paradigm can be quite unexpected and occur more frequently than anticipated/desired. In a sense, this seems to be aggravated when the involved repertoire is not intrinsically concept model-centric, such as in the case of RLBI. By way of background, Table III provides a simple depiction of: (1) "Monotonic," which denotes when an increase or decrease at one variable can segue to a corresponding change at the same rate (i.e., linear monotonic) or a different change of rate (i.e., non-linear monotonic) at the other variable, and (2) "Non-monotonic," which denotes when the ML model can alter direction at various points, such as when the first derivative switches signs (i.e., "a sign-changing first derivative") [20]. These are mapped against "Linear," wherein "the output is proportional to the input" and "Non-Linear," wherein the "relationship is more complex" (e.g., the relationship between/among the features is complex, the boundary areas are ambiguous, etc.) [21].

TABLE III. EXEMPLAR RESULTANTS AND MNTZ I&E

	Monotonic		*Non-monotonic*
Linear			
Non-linear			

The Monotonic/Non-monotonic and Linear/Non-linear resultants have varying degrees of I&E for the various complexities. The color coding for Table II utilizes the Red-Orange-Yellow-Green (ROYG) color coding schema, wherein the various shades of colors denote lowest to highest I&E. By way of example, red denotes low, orange denotes low/medium, yellow denotes medium, and green denotes high I&E. The shown boundary areas reflect the approximate encountered I&E, and as depicted in Table II, monotonic can be linear or non-linear. The crossing of "Linear Non-monotonic" is hatched, as technically, it cannot be linear (yet, over the long-term, a near-steady-state oscillation may appear, depending upon the magnification, so as to be quasi-linear); as Nicolaou points out, "in network systems, however, even at the level of linear dynamics, fundamental questions remain open concerning such transient growth — or, more generally, non-monotonic dynamics" [22].

B. The Spawning of NP-Hard Non-Monotonic, Non-Polynomial, and Non-Continuous Functions within and abutting the MNTZ

For the case of the RWS AIS/AICDS-related ML discussed herein, the spawning of "non-monotonic, non-polynomial, and even non-continuous functions" is not infrequent [23]. In other words, within the MNTZ, it is even more challenging to discern/ascertain what the I&E situation will be, for there is an even greater propensity for spawning to the NP-Hard side. This is not dissimilar to the paradigm, wherein the transformation of "non-convex Mixed Integer Non-Linear Programming (MINLP) to convex problems, often spawn further non-convex MINLP problems" that necessitate further handling, as is shown in Figure 3 [2]. In the context of Monotonic/Non-Monotonic and Linear/Non-linear, this is recast, as shown in Figure 4, wherein Non-Monotonic can be Continuous or Discontinuous, and Non-Linear can be Polynomial (e.g., which involves certain operations, such as addition, subtraction, and multiplication as well as non-negative integers as powers) or Non-Polynomial (e.g., wherein other operations are possible, and powers can be negative, fractional, or trigonometric, etc.).

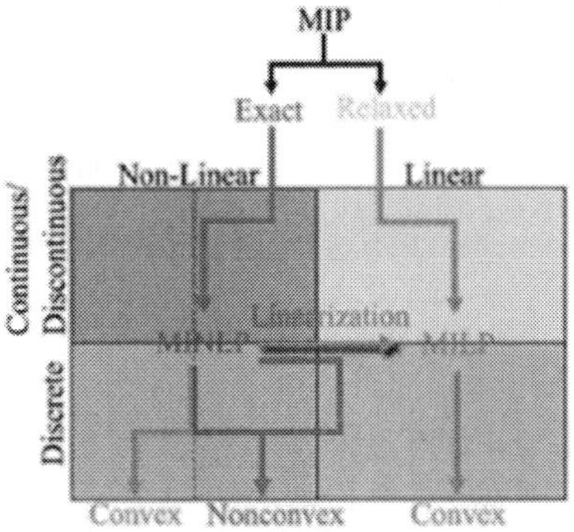

Figure 3. Non-convex to convex transformation pathways (e.g., non-convex discontinuous non-linear MINLPs to convex form)

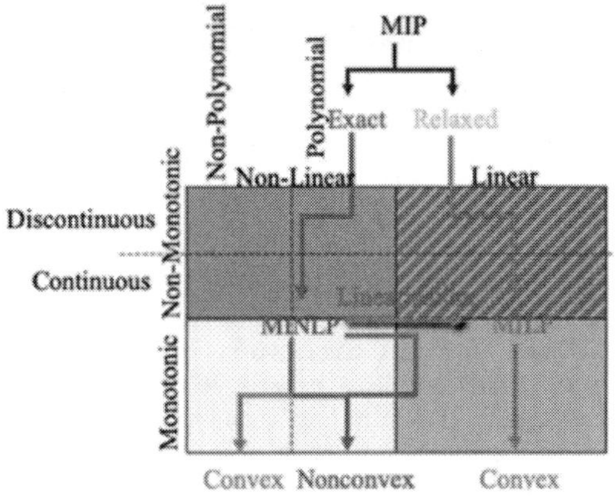

Figure 4. Non-convex to convex transformation pathways (e.g., non-convex non-monotonic, non-polynomial, non-continuous MINLPs to convex form)

Figure 3 and Figure 4 depict the pathways to convex form (e.g., linearization) in green font; once in a convex form, a myriad of Semi-Definite Programming (SDP) solvers can be brought to bear so as to resolve the involved optimization problems in polynomial time (presuming further spawning does not occur). In both cases, NP-hard-related spawn can potentially congest matters with an indefinite impasse.

C. Potentially, RLBI Aggravates & RNLBI Alleviates Matters in the MNTZ

RLBI potentially aggravates matters within the AIS MNTZ since its non-concept model-centric paradigm can potentially run counter to the overall construct by inducing increased ambiguity, increasing uncertainty regarding the estimated parameter class, and increasing the likelihood for spawning to the NP-hard, non-continuous, non-polynomial, and non-monotonic side. RNLBI, such as SD, involves a higher level of abstraction-level thinking that is more intrinsically akin to the ultimate notion/abstract concept to be expressed/articulated.

To summarize this section, the MNTZ must be treated for mission-critical RWS AIS/AICDS, as the transition of involved variables from a monotonic to a non-monotonic state can be quite unpredictable and occur at a higher frequency than anticipated/desired. In addition, without apropos mitigation bulwarks, the computational challenge may be inadvertently increased, as the spawning of "non-monotonic, non-polynomial, and even non-continuous functions" can occur at a higher than anticipated/desired rate. Moreover, a number of RWS, such as CAI, may not robustly distinguish between RLBI and RNLBI; this may be of detriment, as RLBI has been observed to potentially negatively impact matters within the AIS/AICDS MNTZ.

III. EXPERIMENTATION

As a Bottom Line Up Front (BLUF) of the main outcome of this section, the experimental findings allude to a paradigm of decreased spawning as relates to RNLBI over RLBI. This should be of no great surprise, as RNLBI tends to be comprised of less subjective facets while RLBI tend to be comprised of inherently subjective elements (e.g., as respondents may construe the various scale points in a number of ways, thereby segueing to a set of data that is more difficult to compare and contrast). The logical progression that leads to these findings is presented as subsections A through B below.

A. Theoretical Foundations & Precursor Experimentation

As noted previously in Section IB, the issue of the quantification of joint contributions is non-trivial. Even taking the more simplistic case of RLBI, there may be a non-monotonic relationship between variables; for example, as one of the measured variables increases/decreases, the other variable may exhibit a complex curve, which may be challenging for I&E. Even for the seemingly simplistic case of the null hypothesis, wherein there exists no relationship between the two variables, it may be challenging to discern/affirm this paradigm. Of course, a monotonic linear relationship is more suitable for I&E. The task of I&E becomes increasingly challenged with a monotonic non-linear relationship, wherein the two variables increase/decrease, but at different rates of change. As discussed in Section IIA, while non-monotonic, technically, cannot be linear, linear dynamics can indeed transiently segue to non-monotonic dynamics, as Nicolaou points out [22]. This transient nature can be better understood via phase transitions, and to better ascertain when the segueing to non-monotonic non-linear paradigms occurs, various measures for monotonic/non-monotonic and linear/non-linear paradigms are utilized, such as presented and described in Table IV below. These Table IV measures are then sorted and presented by exemplar usage in Table V below and on the following page.

TABLE IV. VARIOUS MEASURES FOR MONOTONIC/NON-MONOTONIC AND LINEAR/NON-LINEAR PARADIGMS

Measure	***Descriptor***
Distance Correlation Coefficient (dCor) [23]	dCor is "better at revealing complex... relationships... compared with other correlation metrics" by "integrating both linear and non-linear dependence" [27].
Hoeffding's D Correlation Coefficient (D) [23][24]	D can reflect a certain degree of concordance and discordance.
Information Coefficient of Correlation (ICC) [25]	ICC can provide a gauge of alignment between the posited and actual value.
Kendall's Tau Correlation Coefficient (tau) [23][26]	Tau can illuminate correlations of import when the distributions of the sample set and population are not necessarily known.
Maximal Correlation (MC) [25]	MC pertains to transformations of the data, which are considered to maximize the correlation.
Maximum Information Coefficient (MIC) [25]	MIC encompasses both linear and nonlinear correlations between the "variable pairs."
Mutual Information (MI) [25]	MI is a paradigm, wherein one of the variables conveys a quantifiable amount of information about the other.
Pearson's [Product]-Moment Correlation Coefficient (PPMCC) [23]	PPMCC measures the relationship strength and direction between the "variable pairs."
Percentage Bend Correlation Coefficient (PBCC) [23]	PBCC refers to a paradigm, wherein a specified percentage of marginal observations deviating from the median are weighted downward [28].
Spearman's Rho Correlation Coefficient (rho) [23][26]	Rho scrutinizes the dependence between two random variables [29].

TABLE V. EXEMPLAR USAGE OF VARIOUS MEASURES

		Monotonic	***Non-monotonic***
Linear		D [23] rho [23] tau [23][26] PPMCC [23][25][26] PBCC [23] dCor [23]	N/A[2]
Non-linear		PPMCC[1] [23][25][26] rho [23] tau [23][26] PBCC [23] dCor [23] D [23]	MC[3] [25] dCor[4] [23] D [23] PPMCC[5] [23][25] rho[5] [23][25]

	Curvilinear	rho [23] PBCC [23] dCor [23] PPMCC[4][23] tau [23]	dCor [23] D [23] PPMCC[5] [25] rho[5] [23][25]

[1] Heuvel notes the efficacy of PPMCC with "families of bivariate distribution functions with non-linear monotonic associations" [26].
[2] as noted previously in Section IIA, technically, non-monotonic cannot be linear; however, as noted by Nicolaou, linear dynamics may experience transient segueing "toward non-monotonic dynamics" [22].
[3] requires "greater than 100 observations" [25].
[4] requires "less than 50 observations," as "it is not susceptible to the exact number of observations" [25].
[5] of note, it does not "find non-monotonic dependence," given symmetry [25].

Generally speaking, the reflected ROYG results align with the findings of Mirtagioglu. For example, the following seem to hold: (1) "in cases where there is no relationship between the variables" (e.g., non-functional relationship, wherein "there is no function of one variable that interacts with the other and vice versa"), dCor, D, tau, PPMCC, PBCC, and rho "have given very satisfactory results," as well as MC, (2) "very low values (close to 0)" of rho, tau, PPMCC, and PBCC is emblematic of a "random relationship between the variables," and (3) "very low values (close to 0)" of tau, PPMCC, and PBCC, and rho when conjoined with "very high values (close to 1)" of dCoR is emblematic of a non-monotonic relationship between/among variables, such as shown in Table VI below [23][26].

TABLE VI. EXEMPLAR FINDINGS FROM MEASURES & POSITS

Close to 0	*Close to 1*	*Close to -1*	*Relationship Posits*
dCor, D, tau, PPMCC, PBCC, rho	N/A	N/A	None
rho, tau, PPMCC, PBCC	N/A	N/A	Random
N/A	rho, PPMCC	N/A	Strong Positive Monotonic
N/A	N/A	rho, PPMCC	Strong Negative Monotonic
tau, PPMCC, PBCC, rho,	dCor	N/A	Non-monotonic

The results also somewhat align with the findings of Fujita, Rainio, and Heuvel. However, the rankings and sortings, such as offered by Mirtagioglu (M), Rainio (R), and Heuvel (H) somewhat differ, as shown in Table VII below.

TABLE VII. POSITED RANKING/SORTINGS BY M, R, AND H

	M [23]	*R* [25]	*H* [26]
Linear Monotonic	rho PBCC PPMCC dCor tau	PPMCC[1] rho[2] tau[2]	PPMCC MIC
Non-linear Monotonic	rho PBCC dCor tau D	rho tau PPMCC	PPMCC MIC
Non-linear (e.g., curvilinear)	dCor D	N/A	PPMCC[3] rho[3]
Non-monotonic			MIC

[1] more oriented for "linear association" [26].
[2] more oriented for "monotonic association [26].
[3] however, this is N/A when the non-monotonic dependence is symmetric [25].

Of course, it would be ideal to first, ascertain the involved relationships (initial foray), second, apply the pertinent measures (verification/discernment), and then, perhaps, third, repeat this process recursively; however, this may not always be possible, as there are a number of subtleties/challenges amidst varying temporal conditions/constraints. In any case, the notional construct utilized is shown in Figure 5 on the following page. Furthermore, the exemplar organization and sequencing of the measures (a.k.a., Verification/Discernment or VD measures) of Figure 5 for monotonic transformation and MNTZ insights was treated with the various methods reflected in Table VIII, which applied specific methods (a.k.a., Sorting/Ranking or SR methods) to the VD measures of Figure 5.

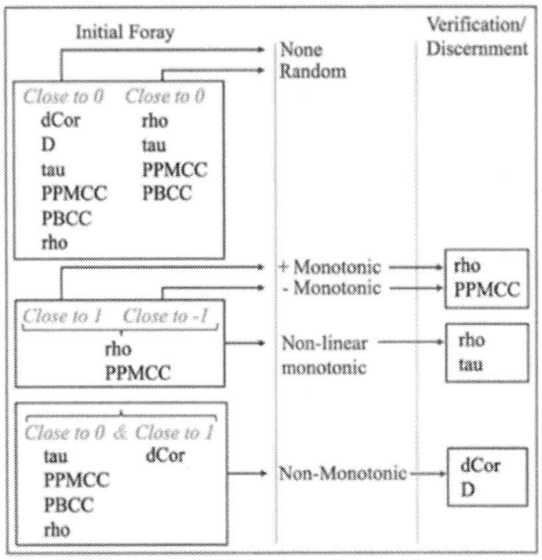

Figure 5. Exemplar sequencing regarding verifications/discernments for monotonic transformation/MNTZ insights

Specifically, the VD measures are needed for more robust insights into the monotonic transformations and ensuing monotonic/non-monotonic dynamics within/around the MNTZ. It should be noted that the SR methods were utilized in a MADM OM sense, since some of the methods are able to handle both SM and OM. As part of the experimentation, a bespoke experimental architectural construct was explored with the OM#1-7 of Table VIII as well as Figures 6 and 7. MULTIMOORA (MM), Goal Programming (GP), and Weighted Aggregated Sum Product Assessment (WASPAS) were presets utilized for MODM SM, MODM OM, and MADM SM, respectively, as shown in Figures 6 and 7 on the following page.

TABLE VIII. METHODS APPLIED TO THE VD MEASURES OF FIGURE 5.

#	*Methods*	*MADM*	*OM*
1	Complex Proportional Assessment (COPRAS)	[30]	[36]
2	CRiteria Importance through Intercriteria Correlation (CRITIC)	[31]	[37]
3	Data Envelopment Analysis (DEA)	[32]	[38]
4	ELimination Et Choix Traduisant la Realité (ELECTRE)	[33]	SM/OM [39]
5	Fuzzy VIseKriterijumska Optimizacija I Kompromisno Resenje (F-VIKOR)	[34]	SM/OM [40]
6	Preference Ranking Organization Method for Enrichment Evaluation (PROMETHEE) (e.g., I and II)	[35]	SM/OM [41]
7	Technique of Order Preference by Similarity to an Ideal Solution (TOPSIS)	[34]	[42]

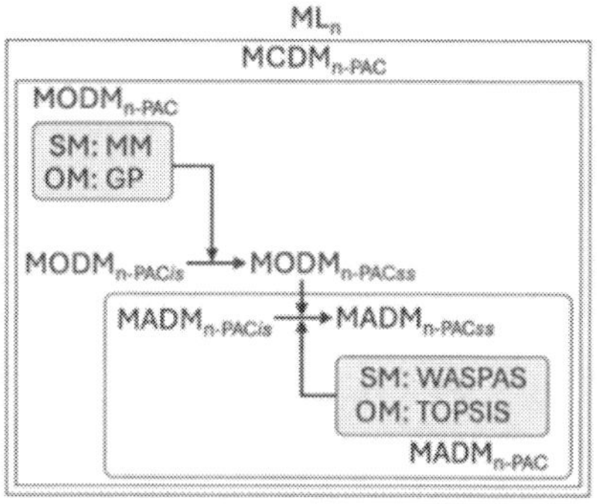

Figure 6. PAC with TOPSIS usage for the MADM OM

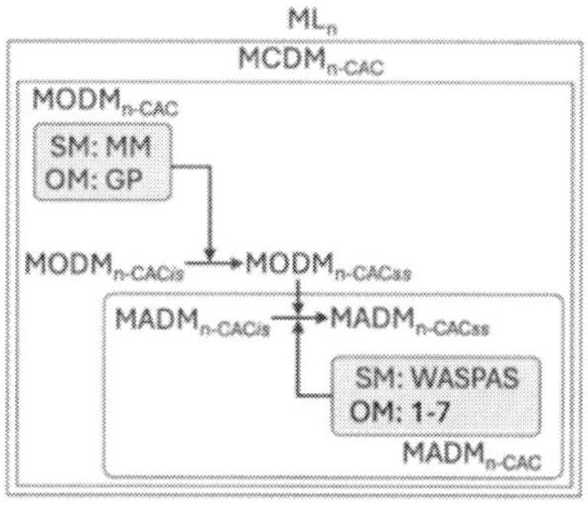

Figure 7. CAC with explicit OM#1-7 usage for MADM

For Figure 6, "PAC" refers to "Previous Architectural Construct," "*is*" equates to "input set," and "*ss*" equates to "solution set." Please note: the "MODM 'solution set' (MODMn-PAC$_{ss}$) facilitates the MADM 'input set' (MADMn-PAC$_{is}$) to MADM 'output solution set' (MADMn-PAC$_{ss}$) progression [2]. For Figure 7, "CAC" refers to "Current Architectural Construct," "*is*" equates to "input set," and "*ss*" equates to "solution set." Please note: the "MODM 'solution set' (MODMn-CAC$_{ss}$) facilitates the MADM 'input set' (MADMn-CAC$_{is}$) to MADM 'output solution set' (MADMn-CAC$_{ss}$) progression [2].

Taking the 7 metrics of **P**erformance (***P***) (i.e., execution time), **C**onsistency (***C***) ("which is a useful indicator" for stability as well as "the underlying convergence paradigm"), **F**lexibility (***F***) ("for adaptation, hybridization, etc."), **S**ensitivity (***S***), *P* under **U**ncertainty (***U***), **V**alidity (***V***), and **I**nterpretability (***I***), various comparative evaluations of OM#1-7 were conducted, and the interim findings are delineated in Figure 8 [43]. For ease of comparison, the relative values were normalized. In terms of benchmarking indicators, Inverted Generational Distance (IGD) and Hypervolume (HV) were utilized, where in the context of the multi-objective domain (e.g., MCDM, MODM, etc.), IGD is a metric that assesses the solution set quality by way of measures, such as convergence (distance of the solutions in the solution set to the Pareto front) and diversity (coverage by the solution set relating to the Pareto front), among others, and HV pertains to the volume of a hv-dimensional space populated by the solution set, where a higher HV alludes to a more robust solution set. This is consistent with Sun and Chugh opining that IGD "has been widely considered as a reliable performance indicator," and likewise, that HV "is one of the most used set-quality indicators" [44][45][46].

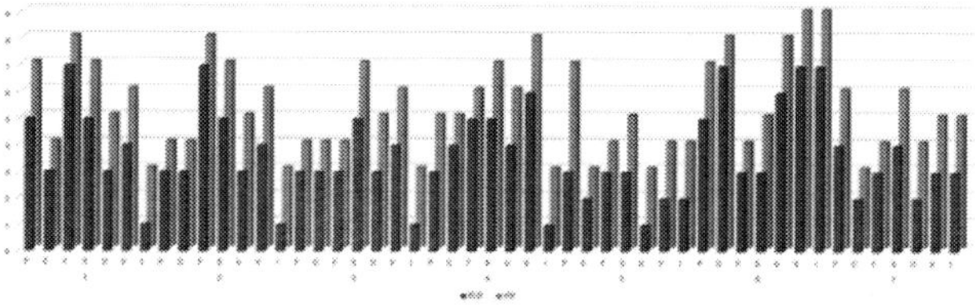

Figure 8. Preliminary Results from OM Benchmarking against IGD/HV

A literature review was conducted to ensure that the results were reasonable, and some example affirmations are shown in Table IX below.

TABLE IX. SAMPLE AFFIRMATIONS OF REASONABLENESS OF RESULTS

Metric	*Exemplar Affirmation*
P	• Varatharajulu favors the COPRAS/TOPSIS amalgam [47]. • Hezer favors COPRAS, TOPSIS, and VIKOR (in that order) [48].
C	• Salabun favors TOPSIS and PROMETHEE over VIKOR [49]. • Ezhilarasan favors ELECTRE over TOPSIS [50][51].
F	• Akram favors extensions of ELECTRE and TOPSIS [52].
S	• Kokaraki opines that TOPSIS may likely be the "most sensitive" (i.e., a high *S*) [53].
U	• Jordehi and Lofti favor ELECTRE [54][55]. • Ziemba favors PROMETHEE [56]. • Taherdoost, Oubahman, and Moreira favor PROMETHEE (e.g., PROMETHEE I for "partial ranking," and PROMETHEE II for "complete ranking"), as it can "accommodate complex qualitative and quantitative evaluations" [57][58][59]
V	• Ozmen favors PROMETHEE to ELECTRE [60].
I	• Leyva-Lopez and Yedjour favor ELECTRE and PROMETHEE [61][62].

Variables and parameters were established as suggested in [45][63].

B. *Updated Experimental Setup*

Initial experimentation had been predicated upon exemplar sample size recommendations, such as shown in Table X, rooted in Gunawan's work, and predicated upon Thompson's *Exploratory and Confirmatory Factor Analysis* [64][65][66].

TABLE X. EXEMPLAR SAMPLE SIZE RECOMMENDATIONS

Recommended Sample Sizes	***Investigators***
200-300	Guadagnoli & Velicer [70]
>=200	Hair et al. [71]
>=200-1000	Nevitt & Hancock [72]
300	Comrey & Lee [67]; Clark & Watson [73]; VanVoorhis & Morgan [74]; White [75]
>=300 is deemed "good enough" (e.g., sample sizes < 300 "tend to diverge") [64][66] [68][69]	Kyriazos & DeVellis [68][69]
>=400	Aleamoni [76]
500 is "very good" [64][67]	Comrey & Lee [67]
>=1,000 is "excellent"	Gunawan [64]; Comrey & Lee [67]

Initially, experimentation sample sizes, such as >=300, were deemed to be sufficient. However, according to Columbia University's Professor Gelman, it is opined that *"you need 16 times the sample size to estimate an interaction than to estimate a main effect"* [77]. As the MNTZ are likely rife with these described *interactions*, Gelman's point is taken. Also, Gelman's argument seems to dovetail with Rainio's thoughts on *power* (e.g., the efficacy to ascertain whether there is "some association between the variables or not"), *equitability* (e.g., the ability to ascertain "similar values for…relationships that are based on different functions but have the same level of noise"), and *generality* (e.g., the capability, at the involved sample quantity, to not only "detect linear, monotonic, or functional dependence," but also "recognize more complicated relationships between the variables") [25]. Interestingly, with an updated experimental setup predicated upon Gelman's and Rainio's thoughts, the findings allude to a paradigm of decreased spawning with RNLBI over RLBI. The pathways discussed within are summarized in Figure 9.

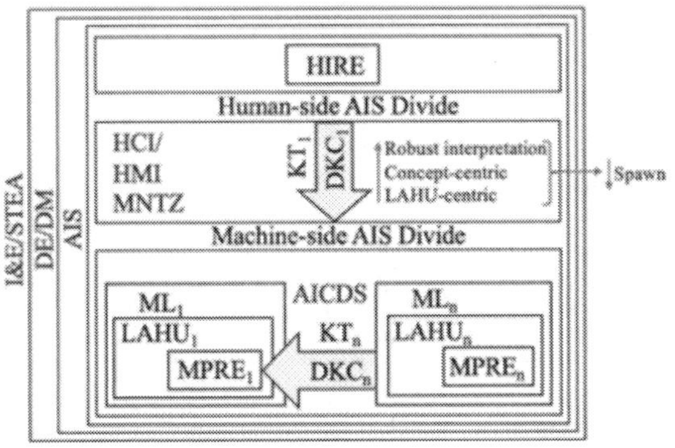

Figure 9. Overall MNTZ and spawn reduction observations/posits

Beyond the pathways, it might be fitting to also address certain aspects of the HIRE human-side and MPRE machine-side of the AIS Divide, particularly as pertains to prospective human-centric and machine-centric (i.e., AI-centric) biases. For example, human respondents might tend to agree with the crowd in the form of acquiescence bias; likewise human respondents might also avoid the extremes and tend towards the "safety" of the "middle of the scale" in the form of central tendency bias. Conversely, the machine might accentuate a particular historical bias and perpetuate that aspect (predicated upon the potentially specious notion that the temporal span of the historical data, albeit possibly biased, carries weight), and interestingly, this might be a long-tail perspective that is exacerbated in the form of selection bias; likewise omitted variable bias can occur, if the machine applies enough weighting to the long-tail perspective (as overfitting can also be a source of bias). For these reasons and others, the mitigation measures alluded to in Section I highlight the prospective robustness of RNLBI over RLBI. In addition, the handling/counterpoising of monotonicity/non-monotonicity can be central for RWS, such as CAIR for CAI; after all, monotonoic reasoning presumes that prior assertions should always hold true. In contrast, non-monotonic reasoning allows for revisions predicated upon new information. In this regard, the LAHU/HALU MCDM component is also critical for treating the temporal component, as RWS (such as CAI) applications tend to occur in real-time. By considering the presented machinations and mitigations, a more robust MNTZ discerning/understanding conjoined with the discussed LAHU/HALU MCDM counterpoisings can potentially segue to more graceful management of seeming contradictions, thereby better harmonizing/counterpoising monotonic/non-monotonic paradigms.

IV. DISCUSSION & CONCLUDING REMARKS

Auret put it well more than a decade ago: a "better understanding of process phenomena is dependent on the interpretation of models capturing the relationships between the process variables" [78]. As these relationships are central, Gelman's recommendations were taken into consideration. With this particular perspective, the explorations of this paper indicate that RLBI can likely be a prospective impediment, particularly within or around the MNTZ for concept model-centric AIS. Indeed, it seems that the spawn rate (e.g., the spawning of "non-monotonic, non-polynomial, and even non-continuous functions") for RLBI may be higher than that for RNLBI [23][79]; however, more quantitative and qualitative forays are needed in this regard (e.g., future works). For the mission-critical RWS AIS/AICDS focus of this paper, it was gleaned that an effective ML on ML paradigm necessitates robust STEA/I&E, which can facilitate the assurance of the intended interpretation, such as via the DKC channel, for KT. Nicolaou reminds us that "transient growth offers interesting alternative explanations for behavior usually attributed to nonlinearity, such as ignition dynamics" [22]; given the myriad of varied connotational interpretations (i.e., alternative explanations), enhanced interpretation, via the DKC interpretand, is particularly vital within/around the MNTZ. The DKC, in the case of this paper, is akin to the LCM in that it is more akin to being concept-based. Accordingly, for meaningful KT to occur, the I&E for the utilized hierarchical/non-hierarchical LVM needs to be of sufficient robustness.

HIRE, which is often replete with RLBI, can skew matters for the AIS/AICDS, as it is not intrinsically concept-based. However, RNLBI, such as SD, can intrinsically be more concept-based (e.g., via its bipolar dichotomy and the in-between continuum). With regards to the DKC recognition element, such as via the quasi-isomorphic engine, the various morphisms (e.g., automorphisms, homeomorphisms, diffeomorphisms, symplectomorphisms, etc.) as well as the various subgraph isomorphism relaxations need to be well treated. However, the utilized approach (e.g., robust convex relaxations) can also further spawn further non-convex MINLP problems, so a reduction in spawning is key. Overall, RNLBI seems to lend towards a reduction of this spawning, and given this prospective mitigation approach, the described machinations at/or abutting the DKC, such as within the MNTZ, can mitigate against the various inferences/predictions/posits/insights of the involved AIS. Of note, the intrinsic wherewithal to accommodate both discrete and continuous paradigms is critical. Along this vein, the LAHU/HALU MCDM, which is at the heart of DE/DM, encompasses MODM for "undetermined continuous alternatives" as well as MADM for "discrete alternatives." Axiomatically, these require continuous as well as discrete evaluations, respectively. It then follows that since RLBI do not contain "0," discrete testing is not possible; restated, only continuous distribution testing is possible. On the contrary, RNLBI (e.g., SD) do indeed contain "0" and are able to accommodate both discrete and continuous distribution testing. The preliminary experimental findings seem to affirm that RNLBI lend toward a higher P, C, F, U, V, I and a lower S than RLBI, particularly in and/or around the MNTZ (with less spawn observed).

To conclude, RNLBI are potentially more amenable to higher nuance/insight and seem to warrant further investigation. After all, this particular facet of AIS/AICDS addresses the important AI challenge of how biases and transition zones may potentially affect DE/DM. In particular, the frameworks for LAHU/HALU, ML on ML/DKC/KT, and MNTZ are central for addressing the challenge by facilitating the exploration of AIS behavior within transition zones (e.g., MNTZ) and ML on ML/DKC/KT frameworks. Future work will entail more quantitative investigation (with careful consideration given toward quantitative fallacy, as alluded to by Gelman), and a more extensive AIS/AICDS comparative literature survey with accompanying empirical evaluation will be conducted.

References

[1] "A Renewed Commitment to Excellence: An assessment of the NASA Agency-wide Applicability of the Columbia Accident Investigation Board Report," NASA, Jan. 2004 [Online]. Accessed: Jul. 2025. Available: https://www.nasa.gov/wp-content/uploads/2015/01/55691main_Diaz_020204.pdf.

[2] S. Chan, "AI-Facilitated Dynamic Threshold-Tuning for a Maritime Domain Awareness Module," 2024 IEEE Int. Conf. on Ind. 4.0, Artif. Intell., and Commun. Technol. (IAICT), Jul. 2024, pp. 192-198.

[3] C. Harris, R. Pymar, and C. Rowat, "Joint Shapley values: a measure of joint feature importance," Arxiv.org, Feb. 2022. [Online]. Accessed: Jul. 2025. Available: https://arxiv.org/pdf/2107.11357.

[4] K. Dhamdhere, A. Agarwal, and M. Sundararajan, "The Shapley Taylor Interaction Index," Proc. of the 37th Int. Conf. on Mach. Learn., pp. 9259–9268, Jul. 2020.

[5] A. Winfield, et al, "IEEE P7001: A Proposed Standard on Transparency," Front. Robot. AI, vol. 8, pp. 1-11, Jul. 2021.

[6] M. Wang, L. Zhou, Q. Li, and A. Zhang, "Open world long-tailed data classification through active distribution optimization," Expert Syst. with Appl., vol. 213, Mar. 2023.

[7] Z. Liu, et al., "Large-Scale Long-Tailed Recognition in an Open World," 2019 IEEE/CVF Conf. on Comput. Vision and Pattern Recognit. (CVPR), Jan. 2019, pp. 2532-2541.

[8] K. Akbari, M. Eigruber, and R. Vetschera, "Risk attitudes: The central tendency bias, " EURO J. on Decis. Process., vol. 12, pp. 1-13, Nov. 2023.

[9] D. Sabolic, M. Samuelson, and M. Magzan, "Obtaining and Interpreting Students' Attitudes – Some Methodological Considerations and a Case Study," Strategies, Challenges and, Opportunities for Sustain. in Uncertain Environ., Sep. 2022, pp. 1-7.

[10] O. Friborg, M. Martinussen, and J. Rosenvinge, "Libert-based vs. semantic differential-based scorings of positive psychological constructs: A psychometric comparison of two versions of a scale measuring resilience," Pers. and Individual Differ., vol. 40, pp. 873-884, Apr. 2006.

[11] T. Yasseri and J. Reher, "Fooled by facts: quantifying anchoring bias through a large-scale experiment," J. of Comput. Soc. Sci., vol. 5, pp. 1001-1021, Jan. 2022.

[12] A. Tversky and D. Kahneman, "Judgment under Uncertainty: Heuristics and Biases: Biases in judgments reveal some heuristics of thinking under uncertainty," Sci., vol. 185, pp. 1124-1131, Sep. 1974.

[13] V. Berger, "Risk of selection bias in randomized trials: further insight," Trials, vol. 17, pp. 1-5, Oct. 2016.

[14] M. Downs, K. Tucker, H. Christ-Schmidt, and Janet Wittes, "Some practical problems in implementing randomization," Clin. Trials, vol. 7, pp. 235-245, Jun. 2010.

[15] A. Adoseri, K. Al-Khalifa, and A. Hamouda, "Re-Thinking Data Strategy and Integration for Artificial Intelligence: Concepts, Opportunities, and Challenges," Appl. Sci., vol. 13, pp. 1-33, Jun. 2023.

[16] F. Scarelli, A. Tsoi, and M. Hagenbuchner, "The Vapnik-Chervonenkis dimension of graph and recursive neural networks," Neural Netw., vol. 108, pp. 248-259, Dec. 2018.

[17] S. Chan and P. Nopphawan, "The Brittleness of a Non-Reconfigurable Distribution Network Topology Approach," 8th Int. Conf. on Condition Monit. and Diagnosis (CMD), Dec. 2020, pp. 238-241.

[18] D. Woods, "Resolving the Command-Adapt Paradox: Guided Adaptability to Cope with Complexity," Compliance and Initiative in the Prod. of Safety, pp. 73-87, Feb. 2024.

[19] J. Druce, J. Niehaus, V. Moody, D. Jensen, and M. Littman, "Brittle AI, Causal Confusion, and Bad Mental Models: Challenges and Successes in the XAI Program," Arxiv.org, Jun. 2021. [Online]. Accessed: Jul. 2025. Available: https://arxiv.org/pdf/2106.05506.

[20] M. Pasic, "Strong non-monotonic behavior of particle density of solitary waves of nonlinear Schrodinger equation in Bose-Einstein condensates," Commun. In Nonlinear Sci. and Numer. Simul., vol. 29, pp. 161-169, Dec. 2015.

[21] C. Willy and E. Neugebauer, "The Concept of Nonlinearity in Complex Systems," Eur. J. of Trauma, vol. 29, pp. 11-22, Feb. 2003.

[22] Z. Nicolaou, T. Nishikawa, S. Nicholson, J. Green, and A. Motter, "Non-normality and non-monotonic dynamics in complex reaction networks," Phys. Rev. Res. 2, pp. 1-15, Oct. 2020.

[23] H. Mirtagioglu and M. Mendes, "On Monotonic Relationships," Biostatistics and Biometrics, vol. 10, pp. 1-11, May 2022.

[24] A. Fujita, J. Sato, M. Demasi, "Comparing Pearson, Spearman, and Hoeffding's D measure for gene expression association analysis, "J. of Bioinformatics and Comput. Biology," vol. 7, pp. 663-684, Sep. 2009.

[25] O. Rainio, "Different Coefficients for Studying Dependence," The Indian J. of Stat., vol. 84-B, pp. 895-914, Nov. 2022.

[26] E. Heuvel and Z. Zhan, "Myths About Linear and Monotonic Associations: Pearson's r, Spearman's ρ, and Kendall's τ," The Amer. Stat., vol. 76, pp. 44-52, Nov. 2021.

[27] J. Hou, et al., "Distance correlation application to gene co-expression network analysis," BMC Bioinformatics, vol. 23, pp. 1-24, Feb 2022.

[28] C. Pernet, R. Wilcox, and G. Rousselet, "Robust correlation analyses: false positive and power validation using a new open source Matlab toolbox," Front. Psychol., vol. 3, pp. 1-18, Jan. 2013.

[29] Y. Dodge, "Spearman Rank Correlation Coefficient," In: The Concise Encyclopedia of Statist. New York, NY: Springer, 2008, pp. 502-505.

[30] R. Garg, R. Kumar and S. Garg, "MADM-Based Parametric Selection and Ranking of E-Learning Websites Using Fuzzy COPRAS," IEEE Trans. on Educ., vol. 62, pp. 11-18, Feb. 2019.

[31] A. Lubis, N. Khairina, and M. Riandra, "Comparison between Multiple Attribute Decision Making Methods through Objective Weighting Method in Determining Best Employee," Int. J. of Innov. Res. in Comput. Sci. & Technol. (IJIRCST), vol. 11, pp. 2347-5552, Mar. 2023.

[32] N. Wichapa, A. Choompol, and R. Sangmuenmao, "A novel Full Multiplicative Data Envelopment Analysis Model for solving Multi-Attribute Decision-Making problems," Decis. Anal. J., vol. 14, pp. 1-17, Mar. 2025.

[33] A. Demidovskij, "Comparative Analysis of MADM Approaches: ELECTRE, TOPSIS and Multi-level LDM Methodology," XXIII Int. Conf. on Soft Comput. and Meas. (SCM), Sep. 2020, pp. 190-193.

[34] S. Zolfani, M. Yazdani, D. Pamucar, and P. Zarate, "A VIKOR and TOPSIS focused reanalysis of the MADM methods based on logarithmic normalization," Facta Univ. Ser.: Mech. Eng., vol. 18, pp. 341-355, Apr. 2020.

[35] K. Anupama, S. Gowri, B. Rao and T. Murali, "A PROMETHEE approach for network selection in heterogeneous wireless environment," Int. Conf. on Adv. in Comput., Commun. and Inform. (ICACCI), Dec. 2014, pp. 2560-2564.

[36] J. Roy, H. Sharma, S. Kar, E. Zavadskas, and J. Saparauskas, "An extended COPRAS model for multi-criteria decision-making problems and its application in web-based hotel evaluation and selection," Econ. Res.-Ekonomska Istrazivanja, vol. 32, pp. 219-253, Feb. 2019.

[37] A. Krishnan, M. Kasim, R. Hamid, and M. Ghazali, "A Modified CRITIC Method to Estimate the Objective Weights of Decision Criteria," Symmetry, vol. 13, pp. 1-20, May 31.

[38] M. Taleb, R. Khalid, R. Ramli, M. Ghasemi, and J. Ignatius, "An integrated bi-objective data envelopment analysis model for measuring returns to scale," Eur. J. of Oper. Res., vol. 296, pp. 967-979, Feb. 2022.

[39] L. Vasto-Terrientes, A. Valls, R. Slowinski, and P. Zielniewicz, "ELECTRE-III-H: An outranking-based decision aiding method for hierarchically structured criteria," Expert Syst. with Appl., vol. 42, pp. 4910-4926, Jul. 2015.

[40] Y. Suh, Y. Park, and D. Kang, "Evaluating mobile services using integrated weighting approach and fuzzy VIKOR," PloS One, vol. 14, pp. 1-28, Jun. 2019.

[41] M. Basilio, V. Pereira, and F. Yigit, "New Hybrid EC-Promethee Method with Multiple Iterations of Random Weight Ranges: Applied to the Choice of Policing Strategies," Math., vol. 11, pp. 1-34, Oct. 2023.

[42] S. Chakraborty, "TOPSIS and Modified TOPSIS: A comparative analysis," Dec. Anal. J., vol. 2, pp. 1-7, Mar. 2022.

[43] S. Chan, "AI-Facilitated Selection of the Optimal Nondominated Solution for a Serious Gaming Information Fusion Module," IEEE Gaming, Entertainment, and Media Conf. (GEM), Jul. 2024, pp. 1-6.

[44] Y. Sun, G. Yen, and Z. Yi, "IGD Indicator-based Evolutionary Algorithm for Many-objective Optimization Problems," Arxiv.org, Feb. 2018. [Online]. Available: https://arxiv.org/pdf/1802.08792.

[45] T. Chugh, "Scalarizing Functions in Bayesian Multiobjective Optimization," IEEE Congr. on Evol. Comput. (CEC), Sep. 2020, pp. 1-8.

[46] A. Guerreiro, C. Fonseca, and Luis Paquete, "The Hypervolume Indicator: Computational Problems and Algorithms," ACM Comput. Surv., vol. 54, pp. 1-42, Jul. 2021.

[47] M. Varatharajulu, M. Duraiselvam, M. Kumarr, G. Jayaprakash, N. Baskar, "Multi criteria decision making through TOPSIS and COPRAS on drilling parameters of magnesium AZ91," J. of Magnesium and Alloys, vol. 10, pp. 2857-2874, Oct. 2022.

[48] S. Hezer, E. Gelmez, E. Ozceylan, "Comparative analysis of TOPSIS, VIKOR and COPRAS methods for the COVID-19 Regional Safety Assessment," J. Infect. Public Health, vol. 14, pp. 775-786, Mar. 2024.

[49] W. Salabun, J. Watrobski, and A. Shekhovtsov, "Are MCDA Methods Benchmarkable? A Comparative Study of TOPSIS, VIKOR, COPRAS, and PROMETHEE II Methods," Uncertain Multi-Criteria Optim. Problems, vol. 12, pp. 1-56, Sep. 2020.

[50] Rivensin, "TOPSIS and ELECTRE Comparison Analysis on Web-based Software," J. Ilmiah Kursor, vol. 11, pp. 33-42, Jul. 2021.

[51] N. Ezhilarasan and A. Felix, "Fuzzy ELECTRE AND TOPSIS method to analyze the risk factors of tuberculosis," J. Phys.: Conf. Ser., vol. 2267, pp. 1-23, May 2022.

[52] M. Akram, H. Garg, and K. Zahid, "Extensions of ELECTRE-I and TOPSIS methods for group decision-making under complex Pythagorean fuzzy environment," Iranian J. of Fuzzy Syst., vol. 17, pp. 147-164, May 2020.

[53] N. Kokaraki, C. Hopfe, E. Robinson, and E. Nikolaidou, "Testing the reliability of deterministic multi-criteria decision-making methods using building performance simulation," Renewable and Sustain. Energy Rev.," vol. 112, pp. 991-1007, Sep. 2019.

[54] A. Jordehi, "How to deal with uncertainties in electric power systems? A review," Renewable and Sustain. Energy Rev., vol. 96, pp. 145-155, Nov. 2018.

[55] F. Lotfi, T. Allahviranloo, W. Pedrycz, M. Shahriari, H. Sharafi, and S. GhalehJough, "Elimination Choice Translating Reality (ELECTRE) in Uncertainty Environment," Stud. in Comput. Intell., vol. 1121, pp. 179-214, Nov. 2023.

[56] P. Ziemba, "Uncertainty of Preferences in the Assessment of Supply Chain Management Systems Using the PROMETHEE Method," Symmetry, vol. 14, pp. 1-16, May 2022.

[57] H. Taherdoost and M. Madanchain, "Using PROMETHEE Method for Multi-Criteria Decision Making: Applications and Procedures," Iris J. of Econ. & Bus. Manage., pp. 1-7, May 2023.

[58] L. Oubahman and S. Duleba, "Review of PROMETHEE method in transportation," Prod. Eng. Arch., vol. 27, pp. 1-6, Mar. 2021.

[59] M. Moreira, C. Dupont and M. Vellasco, "PROMETHEE and Fuzzy PROMETHEE Multicriteria Methods for Ranking Equipment Failure Modes," 15th Int. Conf. on Intell. Syst. Appl. to Power Syst., Dec. 2009, pp. 1-6.

[60] E. Ozmen and B. Demir, "The analysis of risk assessment for the transmission of COVID-19 by using PROMETHEE and ELECTRE methods," Sigma J. of Eng. and Natural Sci., vol. 41, pp. 232-242, Apr. 2023.

[61] J. Leyva-Lopez, J. Solano-Noriega, J. Rodriguez-Castro, and P. Sanchez, An Estension of the ELECTRE III Method based on the 2-tuple Linguistic Representation Model for Dealing with Heterogeneous Information," Comput. Y. Syst., vol. 28, pp. 1-23, Sep. 2024.

[62] D. Yedjour, H. Yedjour, M. Amri, and A. Senouci, "Rule extraction based on PROMETHEE-assisted multi-objective genetic algorithm for generating interpretable neural networks," Appl. Soft Comput., vol. 151, Jan. 2024.

[63] S. Huband, L. Barone, L. While, and P. Hingston, "A scalable multi-objective test problem toolkit," Int. Conf. on Evol. Multi-Criterion Optim., 2005, pp. 280–295.

[64] J. Gunawan, C. Marzilli, and. Y. Aungsuroch, "Establishing appropriate sample size for developing and validating a questionnaire in nursing research," Belitung Nurs. J., vol. 7, pp. 356-360, Oct. 2021.

[65] W. Chen, L. McLeod, T. Coles, "Rasch First? Factor First," ISPOR 17th Ann. Eur. Congr., Amsterdam, The Netherlands, Nov. 2014, pp. 1-2.

[66] B. Thompson, Exploratory and Confirmatory Factor Analysis: Understanding concepts and applications, Washington DC, U.S.: APA, 2004, pp. 1-218.

[67] A. Comrey and H. Lee, A first Course in Factor Analysis, 2nd ed., New York, NY, U.S.: Psychology Press, 1992, pp. 1-142.

[68] A. Dayimu, N. Simidjievski, N. Demiris, and J. Abraham, "Sample size determination for prediction models via learning-type curves," Statist. in Med., vol. 43, pp. 1-11, May 2024.

[69] R. Kumar and S. Singal, "Penstock material selection in small hydropower plants using MADM methods," Renewable and Sustain. Energy Rev., vol. 52, pp. 240-255, Dec. 2015.

[70] E. Guadagnoli and W. Velicer, "Relation of sample size to the stability of component patterns," Psychol. Bull., vol. 103, pp. 265-275, Mar. 1988.

[71] J. Hair, B. Black, B. Babin, and R. Anderson, "Overview of Multivariate Methods," in Multivariate Data Anal., 7th ed, London: Pearson Hall, 2010, ch. 1, pp. 1-785.

[72] J. Nevitt and G. Hancock, "Performance of bootstrapping approaches to model test statistics and parameter standard error estimation structural equation modeling," Struct. Equ. Model., vol. 8, pp. 353-377, Nov. 2009.

[73] L. Clark and D. Watson, "Constructing validity: Basic issues in objective scale development," in Methodological issues and strategies in clinical research, 4th ed., A. E. Kazdin (Ed.), Washington DC, U.S.: APA, 2016, pp. 187-203.

[74] C. VanVoorhis and B. Morgan, "Understanding the Power and Rules of Thumb for Determining Sample Sizes," Tut. in Quantitative Methods for Psychol., vol. 3, pp. 43-50, Sep. 2007.

[75] M. White, "Sample size in quantitative instrument validation studies: A sytematic review of articles published in Scopus, 2011," Heliyon, vol. 8, pp. 1-6, Dec. 2022.

[76] L. Aleamoni, "The relation of sample size to the number of variables in using factor analysis techniques," Educ. and Psychol. Meas., vol. 36, pp. 879-883, Dec. 1976.

[77] A. Gelman, "Statistical Modeling, Causal Inference, and Social Science," Columbia Univ., Nov. 2023. [Online]. Accessed: Jul. 2025. Available: https://statmodeling.stat.columbia.edu/2023/11/09/you-need-16-times-the-sample-size-to-estimate-an-interaction-than-to-estimate-a-main-effect-explained/.

[78] L. Auret and C. Aldrich, "Interpretation of nonlinear relationships between process variables by use of random forests," Minerals Eng., vol. 31, pp. 27-42, Aug. 2012.

[79] P. Hall, S. Ambati, and W. Phan, "Ideas on interpreting machine larning," O'Reilly, Mar. 2017. [Online]. Accessed: Jul. 2025. Available: https://www.oreilly.com/radar/ideas-on-interpreting-machine-learning/.

Learner Models:

Requirements and Legal Issues for the Development and Application of Learner Models

Felix Böck[1] [0000-0001-7382-8333], Hendrik Link[2] [0009-0006-0596-2120] and Dieter Landes[1] [0000-0002-0741-3540]

[1] Center for Responsible Artificial Intelligence (CRAI),
Coburg University of Applied Sciences and Arts, 96450 Coburg, Germany
{felix.boeck, dieter.landes}@hs-coburg.de
[2] Public Law, IT Law, and Environmental Law,
University of Kassel, 34109 Kassel, Germany
hendrik.link@uni-kassel.de

Abstract — **Learners differ vastly in various aspects of what they need for successful learning. Artificial Intelligence (AI) establishes a basis for digital learning environments which adapt themselves automatically to the learners' needs. To be able to do so, these systems presuppose knowledge on the individual learner. Learner models are digital representations of learner characteristics that aim to enable personalised and adaptive learning experiences, touching upon issues in key areas, such as transparency, fairness, data protection, modularity, and sustainability. Such learner models form the core of AI-based adaptive learning environments, as they store data about individual learners. This paper collects and discusses requirements, legal issues, and challenges associated with developing and using learner models, particularly in the context of European regulations. By reviewing existing standards, scientific publications, and practical use cases, we identify gaps in standardisation and propose foundational requirements for the design of interoperable and legally compliant learner models. Our findings lay the groundwork for developing a reference architecture, facilitating scalable and ethical integration of learner models in digital learning environments.**

Keywords — learner model; learner modelling; requirements engineering; legal issues; compliance; ethical principles; higher education; learning analytics.

I. INTRODUCTION

Learners tend to be increasingly heterogeneous as a group since they differ in terms of individual levels of knowledge and competencies, learning styles, individual preferences for (digital) media, and various other factors [1][2]. A potential solution to accommodate this growing heterogeneity might be digital learning environments, which supports users in a given situation. This is possible on various levels. In this work, we focus exclusively on learning environments that support learners on the micro level by adapting to their specific needs in self-directed learning. Yet, adaptation presupposes some knowledge of the individual learner, which is usually stored in a learner model (aka user model). The latter constitutes a collection of user characteristics that are relevant for individual learning support [3][4]. Although a vast amount of literature exists on learner models, there seems to be no consensus concerning the content and purpose of a learner model [4] and the legal constraints that restrict the use of the information embedded in the learner model. This contribution identifies requirements that a learner model should fulfil to provide individual learning support. Requirements are derived from a comprehensive analysis of scientific publications [4] and standards on learner models [3]. In addition, we address legal issues related to the development and operation of digital learning environments that rely on personal data of learners. To do so, we take a European perspective. We aim to contribute to identifying common requirements for learner models, which could be implemented in a further step through a reference architecture, considering legal constraints. The remainder of this paper first clarifies the terminology in Section 2, before Section 3 outlines typical usage scenarios of learner models and Section 4 discusses related work. Section 5 presents requirements that are mandatory, desirable, or otherwise relevant for learner models before Section 6 contrasts this with legal considerations based on European laws and regulations. Section 7 summarises the paper and provides an outlook on future research.

II. DEFINITION OF TERMS

This paper views a learner model solely as a digitally processed representation of learners' characteristics [3]. Inference mechanisms and reasoning may refer to a learner model, but are separate components rather than part of the model. Furthermore, learner models need to be distinguished from learning analytics: while the latter involves the analysis of group behaviour to predict individual outcomes, a learner model serves as a basis for tailoring the learning process to individual learners. Both approaches examine behavioural data and derive new insights which, once interpreted, enable the implementation of new measures. Open learner models constitute a notable development since they make model contents accessible to the learner or other parties involved in the learning process, such as teachers or parents. Open learner models are visual representations of machine-readable formats of components of learner models [5]. By offering tools for self-reflection in different formats, learners should be supported in various ways [6]. Learning Analytics Dashboards (*LAD*) share a similar objective [7]. Unlike learner models, LADs rely on a static representation of behavioural metrics derived from interaction data, while learner models focus on modelling knowledge and other individual characteristics of the learner [7][8]. Learner models and learning analytics both require personalised data from learners, which is subject to the same legal principles. Although goals and ways of working differ, the requirements and legal aspects can be pretty similar. Therefore, we also consider learning analytics and examine if specific aspects also apply to learner models, possibly with adaptations. We summarise both approaches and refer to them as learning analyses.

Learning environments are (digital) platforms where learners may use different content via various learning elements to educate themselves independently. Learning environments are not defined further here, as they are sufficient for the context at the meta level. It does not matter whether the learning environment is, e.g., a mobile application, an institutional continuing education platform, or even innovative learning settings with XR.

III. Usage Scenarios

Learner models and adaptation do matter at different levels: from support in planning a degree program [macro level] (which modules are interesting for me?), to learning patterns of student cohorts during their studies [meso level] (which topics prove difficult within certain student cohorts?), to which concepts within a module [micro level]. We will focus mainly on the micro level.

Individual adaption of the learning process is only viable if information and data about the respective learner can be used to respond to the needs of the respective learners and provide them with individualised support. The concept just mentioned will not scale to, e.g., entire study cohorts of degree programmes without further aid. The abundance of learner data, its pre-processing and intelligent aggregation make manual evaluation by the instructor for each individual learner almost impossible, which is why computer-aided methods are usually used. Digital recommendation systems automate the provision of individual support to users for making better decisions [9], often by building upon learner models. Figure 1 visualises the reference workflow of the learning process within a digital learning platform. The starting point is the completion of learning and teaching activities within the digital learning environment. During the learning process, many different types of behavioural data are collected about learners and their activities. This data is pre-processed and then made persistent to enable reproducible analyses subsequently. In addition to behavioural data, other structured knowledge about a learner (such as previous education, learning type, etc.) is also stored and analysed, resulting in individual recommendations for the next learning activities and feedback on previously visited learning elements.

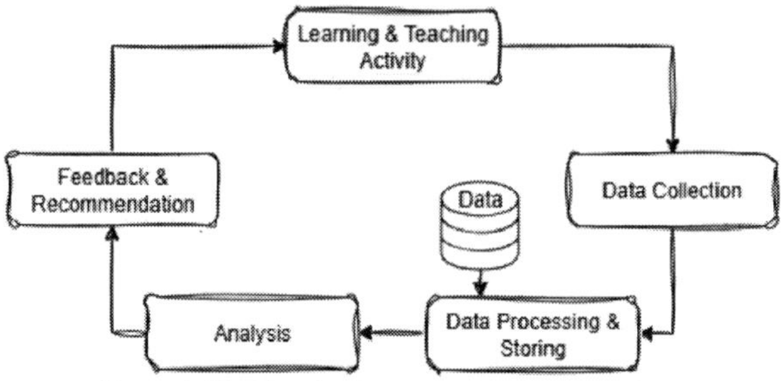

Figure 1. Workflow Reference Architecture (*based on* [10])

The basis for adaptive teaching and learning settings is the learner model, which stores all relevant data persistently and makes it available as required. Yet, the learner model should not be considered in isolation, but in the overall context of the digital learning environment and the associated relationships, as the added value of learner models only comes into play when they are used in the adaptive learning platform. The following section presents examples of typical scenarios from digital teaching to illustrate the specific application purpose. The necessary measures and requirements can then be derived subsequently. These three actors also form the three levels of adaptive learning described above. For the sake of completeness and better understanding, all three are briefly outlined here, although the focus remains on the micro level and thus on the learner.

A. *Purpose of Use*

Several publications, e.g., ISO/IEC JTC1/SC36 [10] or [11][12], already present typical scenarios of digital learning at different levels. Teaching and learning activities in digital learning environments are the starting point for digital learning analyses. Learning analyses are used to personalise and thus improve the learning environment adaptively. Based on the results of the learning analysis, the learning environment can recommend individualised learning paths in combination with distinct learning content. Three main actors are involved in typical learning scenarios: the learner, the instructor, and the educational institution.

Learner (*micro level*). In the past, log entries from the learning environment were difficult to understand for non-technical users, if they could be viewed at all. Nowadays, learners can obtain visual displays of their data in dashboards, e.g., to monitor their learning progress in relation to the average performance of the entire cohort. The early recognition of learners' personal needs and preferences (predictive analytics), including possible performance deficits, and the resulting initiation of preventive remedial measures (timely interventions) increase the effectiveness of the learning process. The use of such learning analyses also contributes to supporting students with disabilities and to identifying accessibility deficits in learning opportunities.

Instructor (*meso level*). Instructors can track activities of their entire cohorts and detect progress and potential problem patterns, e.g., lack of learner engagement, early in the course. Consequently, instructors may initiate appropriate support through adaptive teacher response to observed learner needs and behaviour.

Educational Institution (*macro level*). The educational institution can contribute to an improved holistic individual education strategy through the possibility of analyses, which can also reduce drop-out rates in the long term. In addition, administration may benefit from information on the entire student population, e.g., for future course planning. If comparisons of the data set across learning modules are permitted, similar patterns can be identified, and indications can be derived, such as a potential accessibility problem.

B. Legal Principles and Classification

The implementation of learner models in educational institutions has various legal implications. On the one hand, for example, intellectual property is protected from the developer's perspective. On the other hand, learners' rights, especially their fundamental rights, must be considered. In the EU, the fundamental right to data protection, as stated in Article 8 of the EU Charter of Fundamental Rights (*CFR*) [13], is affected. The specific legal implementation of this fundamental right, the General Data Protection Regulation (*GDPR*) [14], is the primary law to be considered when using learner models. These provisions are considered when determining legal requirements.

IV. Related Work

Learning offers must be modularised so that individual learning paths can be created based on a wide range of criteria. Many publications, particularly in the last decade [4], deal with adaptive teaching and learning settings. For this work, scientific publications on user models, particularly learner models, are the most relevant. Koch [15][16] summarised the seven objectives of a user model: (1) supporting users in learning a specific topic; (2) providing users with customised information; (3) adapting the user interface to the user; (4) supporting users in searching for information; (5) providing users with feedback on their knowledge; (6) supporting collaborative work; (7) supporting the system's use.

Numerous publications deal with learner analyses, although mostly only as a means to the end of adaptive learning systems [17][18] or very superficially, without going into relevant details. Several publications also only consider individual information rather than their aggregation into a learner model [19][20]. A couple of surveys attempt to create an overview of the field [21]-[24], but mostly only compare the different models with each other, without providing direct insight into which learner characteristics can be used, how they are modelled, or where required data comes from. Therefore, we conducted two parallel systematic literature searches on learner models, on the one hand, to get a comprehensive picture of the current state of science research [4] and, on the other hand, to clarify the state of practice based on standards and norms [3]. Ideally, this should pave the way to a standardised approach to how learner models are designed and created, as well as a set of standardised subcomponents – regardless of their purpose and use. 868 standards were reviewed, 16 of which were classified as relevant to the structure and components of learner models. Three standards deal intensively with learner models. Among those, ISO/IEC 29140:2021 [10] describes a mobile learner model that considers specific attributes, such as the device used, connectivity and the learner's location to describe the learning environment better. The 1EdTech consortium [25] focuses on the interoperability of internet-based information systems that support learners in their interaction with other systems. It uses a data model that captures the essential characteristics of learners to monitor and manage their progress, goals, performance, and learning experiences. IEEE P1484.2 [26] attempted to specify the syntax and semantics of a learner model by centralising public and private learner information, which became known as PAPI Learner. This endeavour started in the 1990s, but was not pursued further. Extensive research into norms and standards in the field of learner models has shown that approaches in this area are rare and either specialised [10], complex and more than just learner models [25], or have been abandoned [26]. No standards have been found that describe a generalised realisable learner model that can be extended according to specific use cases or that deal with the creation of such learner models [3].

In parallel, scientific publications of relevant publishers (*IEEE, ACM, Elsevier, pedocs*) from 2014 to 2023 were examined systematically, leading to 197 papers, which were relevant enough to be analysed in detail [4]. Scientific publications on the design and development of learner models reveal a variety of different approaches. Many models integrate characteristics such as learning style, but do not specify why or how these characteristics influence learning and whether or why it makes sense to take them into account. There is also a lack of clear recommendations as to which combinations of characteristics should be included in a learner model. Standardised characteristics, such as demographic data (e.g., name, gender, age), are often used together with behavioural and learning data. The modelling of this data varies greatly in the literature. Knowledge characteristics can be modelled using, e.g., overlay models or fuzzy logic. This diversity makes it hard for developers to make decisions and implement the models. In addition, publications often lack details on data sources, data processing, and practical implementation of model components. Many of these topics are only touched upon in passing or omitted altogether, which makes it difficult to replicate learner models precisely [4].

The two systematic literature searches indicate that the descriptions of learner models are often rather superficial and lack detail. Many explanations refer to frequently used standards and then expand these to include individual aspects [27]-[30][20], but do not describe in detail how these are expanded or what the implementation or modelling of the learner model looks like. Legal implications of learner models, specifically, have not yet been discussed. However, there is research regarding the requirements of the European data protection law in learning analytics, which can also be used for learner models [31]-[36]. So far, proposals are available for the standardisation of leaner models, such as educational metadata or course data. Our main objective is to contribute to this standardisation process with an original proposal for a reference model as one of the first steps towards a reference architecture. This contribution is based on the definition of open software interfaces for each subsystem in the architecture, avoiding any dependency on specific information models. We have already discussed elsewhere a possible reference architecture for an adaptive learning platform which integrates a learner model is [37].

V. Requirements

Based on the previously analysed publications and the resulting findings on possible components of learner models and their use in digital learning environments, we derive a list of requirements for a learner model and its application. The development of the requirements specification is based on a qualitative analysis. In parallel publications, we already dealt with the functional requirements of learner models in greater detail [37] and also focused on the overall context of digital learning environments and the integration of learner models [38]. Based on literature research, the following section will focus on non-functional requirements and the legal basis for the use of learner models in Europe. The following section is by no means comprehensive, but rather collects and summarises the most relevant requirements in terms of their occurrence and description in the literature and links them to current legal restrictions in Europe.

In addition to the analysed publications, the feedback and experiences of students at our university play an essential role. It is important to emphasise again that learner models are structured models without any interference mechanisms [39]. However, it is also necessary to consider and evaluate the effects, i.e., the integration of a learner model into the overall eLearning environment, when considering the requirements for a learner model. The following requirements are classified according to the Kano model [40] into so-called *must-be requirements*, one-dimensional requirements (*should characteristics*) and attractive requirements (*can characteristics*).

A. *Must-be Requirements*

Must-be requirements are essential for the successful use of a learner model in future scenarios and form the basis for its design and subsequent development.

Collection and Management of Learning Data. The collection and aggregation of static and dynamic information about the learner (e.g., knowledge, skills, interests, preferences, behavioural data) is the initial step. The utilisation of data from various sources plays a significant role. In the second step, the collected data must be digitally processed, modelled, and persisted.

Legal Data Protection Requirements. The development and use of learner models raise a range of legal considerations. In particular, rights relating to data ownership under the EU Data Act may become relevant. Moreover, if learner models fall under the definition of artificial intelligence systems according to the AI Act, additional restrictions may apply. This is especially the case when such systems are classified as high-risk (Annex III No. 3(b)/(c)), which would trigger extensive compliance obligations. However, the following section focuses on the most immediately relevant legal framework: The General Data Protection Regulation (GDPR). All data to be collected must at all times be subject to the applicable legal requirements of the *GDPR* [14][41]. This requirement is closely aligned with the legal constraints of designing and creating learner models. What are the applicable legal requirements for data collection, processing and storage? These questions can neither be generalised, nor answered in general terms, but must be legally considered and examined individually, depending on the purpose of use and the data to be collected. The concept of a data trust model might be applicable here: A neutral, trustworthy entity ensures that data is processed and used by the defined data protection guidelines and only accessible by authorised parties.

B. *Should-be Requirements*

Should-be requirements are important prerequisites for making optimal use of the learner model in future scenarios. They represent desirable, yet not mandatory, features that increase the efficiency and flexibility of learner models. These requirements serve as an orientation for further development and improvement of the model.

Transparency / Traceability. The transparency of how the system has reached a result [42] creates the trust and acceptance of certain subordinate recommendations, which form the basis of good support [9]. Therefore, it is desirable for learner models to be transparent in every single step of the process if possible, i.e., from the origin of the data to the individual processing steps the data went through and what consequences this has for the result and its explanation. This is important so that backgrounds and issues, such as discrimination potential [43]-[45] in categorisations are illuminated. Transparency thereby draws on individual decisions so that they can be correctly traced. Traceability is achieved by involving the learner in the process right from the beginning and also by taking a learner-centred approach to the design and development of learner models.

Responsibility. Traceability is closely connected to responsibility. The data that may be collected must be left to the users' choice, considering applicable legal standards. That is, students can decide which data may be logged and persisted. This topic also includes compliance with ethical principles. For the digital domain, this means that if the learning management system displays ethical behaviour patterns, learners expect the system's compliance to any ethical guidelines and principles. Briefly summarised, ethics is the view of moral values and their conception (based on Aristotle's *Nicomachean Ethics* and Immanuel Kant's *Categorical Imperative*).

Fairness & Ethics. Fairness affects many different steps within the learning process. For example, algorithms for decision-making and data processing must be checked for possible biases to ensure equal opportunities for all learners [46][47].

Tamper-proof. The data managed and persisted by learner models must be protected from unauthorised intervention and changes. Any changes need to be logged in a traceable manner. This implies two interlinked requirements, namely that unauthorised data access must be prohibited, and, if access is permitted, changed data shall be checked for plausibility and changes shall be logged for tracking purposes.

C. Can Requirements

Could-be requirements represent possible extensions that might optimise the learner model in certain scenarios through, e.g., additional benefits or improved user experience. If necessary, these requirements can be included in future development phases to increase the flexibility and adaptability of the model.

Openness & Visualisation. Learner models should be open [6][48] to promote metacognitive behaviours, such as self-awareness and self-regulation. This means that students may display and analyse their own instance of a learner model for a better understanding of their learning progress and, e.g., misconceptions [5]. In this way, learners can see their current learning status and progress in any area at any time, compare it with their learning goals, and derive follow-up activities. Various visualisation options [49]-[51] are essential for presenting complex learning data in a clear and concise format to the learner. Different representations of the same data can bring learners closer to the various aspects and clarify them [52]. Leaner models designed in this way are called open learner models [53][54].

Negotiation Options. In addition to the pure visualisation of personal data, some learner models also offer the option of interacting with this data and, for example, negotiating with the model if the data shows inadequacies from the learner's perspective [5][55]. In this way, (open) learner models give learners not only responsibility for their individual data and progress but also human control over their personal data.

Data Minimisation & Sustainability. Only data that is absolutely necessary for adaptation should be collected. Minimising the amount of collected data while maximising the value of the information avoids unnecessary strain on the infrastructure.

Modularity & Flexibility. A largely self-contained modular structure of the component of earner models enables flexibility, for example, to swap the technical infrastructure (learning management system) or to export the learner model and integrate and use it in other environments, for example, if the learner changes university after graduation.

Maintainability & Expandability. The learner model should have a modular structure (see previous requirement) to ease future adjustments or extensions. This offers the learner model a certain degree of secured prospects.

Standardised / Interoperability & Integration. Ideally, the description of learner information is standardised so that it can be easily exported and exchanged between different learning platforms (according to the interoperability defined in [56][57]) through standardised interfaces for data exchange and integration. Standard conformity is essential here, i.e., open standards to ensure compatibility with other systems should be supported. Standardisation also enables cross-platform integration, i.e., the model can be seamlessly integrated into existing learning management systems. As with data minimisation (Art. 5 lit. c GDPR), data portability is also a legal requirement (Art. 20 GDPR).

VI. LEGAL CONSTRAINTS

Legal considerations are crucial in the design and development of learner models, as lawful use is only possible if these regulations are adhered to. In our case, we are specifically concerned with the legal requirements in Europe regarding the collection, use, and evaluation of personal data. Personal data plays a crucial role in enabling adaptive customisation of learning processes. Therefore, all data collected must always comply with the relevant legal requirements (data protection). However, data protection also encompasses other aspects. On the one hand, only data that is strictly necessary for meaningful adaptation should be collected (data minimisation & data economy). On the other hand, data should only be collected if there is a legal basis for it (lawfulness). All the aforementioned legal principles are enshrined in the General Data Protection Regulation (*GDPR* [41]). The collection and aggregation of static and dynamic information about the learner (e.g., knowledge, skills, interests, preferences) must be compliant with the GDPR. The utilisation of data from various sources plays a significant role. In the second step, this collected data must be digitally processed, modelled and persisted. Unfortunately, the GDPR is technology-neutral (recital 15 GDPR), requiring the broad terms it employs to be defined explicitly in the context of learner models. The GDPR's requirements are diverse, and due to the limited availability of case law and literature regarding the GDPR in relation to learner models, these legal obligations cannot yet be determined with a high degree of certainty. It is highly recommended that the local data protection officer be integrated as soon as possible into the process of implementing learner models in educational institutions. Many obligations of the GDPR, for example, the data protection impact assessment in Art. 35 GDPR will be very hard to meet without professional support. This chapter aims to identify potential issues arising from the GDPR and highlight key aspects to consider when designing and implementing a learner model. In providing an overview, we focus on the principles of the GDPR, which are concretised in the GDPR, and the arising issues regarding learner models.

Lawfulness - Legal Bases. Every processing of personal data needs a legal base, as stated in Art. 5 para. 1, Art. 6 para. 1 GDPR. Art. 6 para. 1 lit. a GDPR establishes consent as a legal basis, which must be given voluntarily [58, p. 330]. In hierarchical contexts, such as teaching environments, the GDPR requires a strict interpretation. Learners often depend on lecturers for grading, which may pressure them to agree to the processing of their personal data to align with lecturers' expectations. This exemption is not ubiquitous, though. If the use of a learner model is a voluntary additional offer of the educational institution and is not linked to a specific course, voluntary consent seems possible. For state educational institutions, instead, Art. 6 para. 1 lit. e GDPR serves as the legal basis for data processing when processing is necessary for the performance of a task carried out in the public interest, such as education. However, under Art. 6 para. 3 GDPR, the legal basis of Art. 6 para. 1 lit. e GDPR must be complemented by specific legal provisions by the member states that establish obligations and define tasks. Consequently, instructors must ensure that the applicable legal bases in their national laws include the processing of personal data for educational purposes. General requirements that the GDPR imposes on national law are discussed in [59].

Furthermore, the type and extent of data being processed should be carefully evaluated. On the one hand, this enables an assessment of the risks associated with potential data breaches. On the other hand, it highlights whether special categories of personal data are being processed in the learner model. Processing personal data revealing racial or ethnic origin, political opinions, religious or philosophical beliefs, trade union membership, genetic data, biometric data for uniquely identifying individuals, health data, or information about a person's sex life or sexual orientation is subject to stringent requirements. Under Art. 9 para. 2 lit. g GDPR, alongside the requirements of Art. 6 para. 1 lit. e GDPR, a legal basis in Union or Member State law is required, allowing such processing only if it is necessary for reasons of substantial public interest. Meeting this requirement is particularly challenging for learner models.

Purpose limitation. Developers of learner models must carefully evaluate the potential sources of personal data used for their development and operation. Often, the data is collected for a different purpose — for example, when student exams, initially collected for grading purposes, are fed into learner models. In addition, the subsequent use of data generated by the learner model should undergo careful evaluation. Art. 5 para. 1 lit. b GDPR requires that personal data be collected for specific, explicit, and legitimate purposes and not further processed in ways incompatible with those purposes. However, Art. 6 para. 4 GDPR provides an exception: if the new purpose for processing personal data is not based on the data subject's consent or authorised by Union or Member State law, its compatibility with the original purpose must be assessed using the criteria outlined in Art. 6 para. 4 lit. a – e GDPR. Scientific research, which is what learner models could be part of, is privileged. Art. 5 para. 1 lit. b assumes scientific research is "not be considered to be incompatible with the initial purposes".

Transparency. Transparency is not merely a technical requirement but is also enshrined in Art. 5 para. 1 lit. a GDPR. Personal data shall be processed "in a transparent manner in relation to the data subject [...]." This principle is guaranteed by primary law in Art. 8 para. 2 S. 2 CFR by granting every person "the right of access to data which has been collected concerning him or her [...]." The requirement of transparency is primarily detailed in Art. 12 ff. GDPR. It stipulates that if personal data is collected, the controller must, pursuant to Art. 13 GDPR, inform the data subject about the details outlined in Art. 13 paras. 1 and 2 GDPR at the time of collection. This information must be provided in a privacy statement. It is recommended to explain the system in clear and accessible language in the privacy statement to help learners understand how the learner model functions.

Data Minimisation. Within learner models, various sensitive data will be processed, which is in contrast to the GDPR principle of data minimisation, which allows the processing of personal data only when strictly necessary. The principle does not require minimising the data itself but seeks to limit the connection of data to natural persons, thereby reducing infringements of fundamental rights [60] mn. 96. This takes several technical and organisational measures. First, personal data should be pseudonymised. According to Art. 4 No. 5 GDPR, pseudonymisation is the processing of personal data in such a manner that the personal data can no longer be attributed to a specific data subject without the use of additional information. EDSA provides a detailed guideline for pseudonymisation [61]. As an organisational matter, a role concept should be implemented, which specifies who can access the data collected in the learner model and who can edit this data. For complete guidance on technical and organisational measures according to Art. 25 see [62]. Especially, the scope of people who can undo the pseudonymisation needs to be kept small. Also, the use of a data trustee can be discussed [38]. A data trustee is a neutral third party that acts as a steward for sensitive data, ensuring its secure handling, responsible use, and protection of individuals' privacy while facilitating data-driven innovation.

Storage Limitation. The principle of storage limitation, as outlined in Art. 5 para. 1 lit. e GDPR requires that personal data be retained in a form permitting the identification of data subjects only for as long as necessary to achieve the purposes for which it is processed. Temporal storage limitation is a subset of the overarching principle of necessity [60] mn. 122. Educational institutions and lecturers must determine the appropriate retention period for the data. Developers of learning models must ensure that the complete deletion of students' personal data is technically feasible. Typically, learners' personal data should be deleted once they leave the educational institution. If the data is still supposed to be used for the training of learner models, the link between the data and the individual learners can be erased entirely and irreversibly (anonymisation) [63].

Integrity & Confidentiality. Art. 5 para. 1 lit. f GDPR states that personal data must be "processed in a manner that ensures appropriate security of the personal data, including protection against unauthorised or unlawful processing and against accidental loss, destruction, or damage, using appropriate technical or organisational measures." This principle underscores the importance of systemic data protection. It is primarily implemented through Art. 25 GDPR, "Data protection by design," and Art. 32 GDPR, "Security of processing". Whenever possible, data should be stored in an encrypted format on a trustworthy server, ideally on a server operated by the educational institution. The use of servers in an EU member state is unobjectionable, as the GDPR establishes a uniform standard for data protection across member states. The use of servers outside the EU is possible; however, the transfer of data to such servers must comply with Art. 45 et seq. GDPR, which aims to ensure continuity of the level of data protection [64] mn. 6.

Use of Processors. If an external service provider is engaged in processing personal data on behalf of an institution, the requirements of Art. 28 GDPR must be fulfilled. Processors are required to provide sufficient guarantees that they will implement appropriate technical and organisational measures to ensure compliance with the GDPR. These requirements must be formalised in a contract between the educational institution and the processor. Whenever possible, the processor should store data on servers located within the EU.

No automatic Decision-Making with a Legal Impact. Once the learning model is capable of analysing learners' input, it is likely to be used for grading purposes. However, Art. 22 para. 1 GDPR states that decisions based solely on automated processing, including profiling, which produces legal effects, are prohibited. Art. 22 para. 2 GDPR provides exemptions. Still, these are unlikely to apply to the use of learner models unless a member state establishes a legal basis explicitly permitting automated decision-making and defines suitable measures to safeguard the data subject's rights, freedoms, and legitimate interests.

VII. Conclusion and Future Work

Learning models have great potential to make education more individualised, efficient and equitable, but they are still a long way from being implemented in a standardised and legally compliant manner. The key challenge is to reconcile technical innovations with strict legal requirements, particularly those of the GDPR.

The GDPR sets out only very general and technology-neutral requirements, offering few concrete implementation guidelines for learner models. Due to the lack of case law and specific regulatory guidance, legal obligations for learner models remain vague and difficult to apply in practice. This underscores the need for stronger support from data protection authorities in clarifying how GDPR principles can be operationalised in educational technology contexts.

However, as a first step, any processing of personal data must be based on a valid legal basis — typically either informed consent or a legal authorisation, such as the public task basis for educational institutions. Once the legal basis is clarified, data minimisation and storage limitation should become a primary focus. However, this does not mean that the amount of data per se must be reduced, but rather that the identifiability of individuals must be minimised. Accordingly, techniques such as pseudonymisation and, where feasible, anonymisation should be considered to reduce the risk of privacy breaches.

In addition to the legal regulations, technical and non-legal requirements must also be considered in order to design learner models that are practical and effective. The variety of possible requirements analysed is vast. It has not yet been aggregated in a form that makes it easier for designers and developers of learner models to get started. Open learner models offer users transparency about their data, thereby promoting self-reflection and independent learning. Visualisations of complex data help users understand their learning status and continue working in a targeted manner.

Modular and interoperable structures ensure that learner models can be flexibly integrated and transferred between different learning environments. Maintainability and extensibility allow for long-term adaptation to new learning contexts. Overall, these technical requirements illustrate that a well-designed reference model forms the basis for the practical, transparent and fair design of adaptive learning environments.

Another key priority is transparency and traceability in all processing steps: learners must be able to understand how their personal data is processed, who has access to it, and how the system derives its outputs or recommendations. Only then can trust in adaptive learning technologies be established. In addition, fairness and the avoidance of algorithmic bias ensure that all learners have equal opportunities. These questions must be addressed in the next steps, including the design, implementation, and evaluation of a prototype learner model that complies with the outlined legal requirements.

The next technical steps are to conceptualise the legal constraints described in this publication with the help of the local data protection authority and the functional requirements [37] into a interoperable and legally compliant learning model, then to implement this model and integrate it into the learning platform [38]. This initial prototype must be evaluated and further developed in compliance with the legal conditions so that the needs of learners are met and the learning process is improved in a sustainable and prosperous manner. Even though the legal requirements within the EU on this topic are not easy to understand, further steps could be taken to develop the prototype into a reference model for learner models, which would enable other educational institutions to get started with adaptive learning environments more quickly, as learner models have been proven to make a decisive contribution to accommodate the heterogeneity of learners and support their learning processes individually and sustainably.

Acknowledgment

This work is part of the VoLL-KI project and Komp-HI project and funded by the German Ministry of Education and Research (*Bundesministerium für Bildung und Forschung*) under grants 16DHBKI090 and 16DHBKI073.

References

[1] S. Zhang and S. Wang, 'Modeling Learner Heterogeneity: A Mixture Learning Model With Responses and Response Times', *Front. Psychol.*, vol. 9, p. 2339, 2018.

[2] T. Kärner, J. Warwas, and S. Schumann, 'A Learning Analytics Approach to Address Heterogeneity in the Classroom: The Teachers' Diagnostic Support System', *Tech Know Learn*, vol. 26, no. 1, pp. 31–52, 2021.

[3] F. Böck, D. Landes, and Y. Sedelmaier, 'Learner Models: A Systematic Literature Research in Norms and Standards', in *Proceedings of the 16th International Conference on Computer Supported Education*, Angers, France: SCITEPRESS - Science and Technology Publications, 2024, pp. 187–196.

[4] F. Böck, M. Ochs, A. Henrich, D. Landes, J. Leidner, and Y. Sedelmaier, 'Learner Models: Design, Components, Structure, and Modeling - A systematic Literature Review', *User Modeling and User-Adapted Interaction - The Journal of Personalization Research*, Springer, 2025.

[5] S. Bull and J. Kay, 'Open Learner Models', in *Advances in Intelligent Tutoring Systems*, R. Nkambou, J. Bourdeau, and R. Mizoguchi, Eds., in Studies in Computational Intelligence. Springer, 2010, pp. 301–322.

[6] S. Bull and J. Kay, 'Student Models that Invite the Learner In: The SMILI:() Open Learner Modelling Framework', *International Journal of Artificial Intelligence in Education*, vol. 17, no. 2, pp. 89–120, 2007.

[7] R. Bodily *et al.*, 'Open learner models and learning analytics dashboards: a systematic review', in *Proceedings of the 8th International Conference on Learning Analytics and Knowledge*, Sydney New South Wales Australia: ACM, 2018, pp. 41–50.

[8] J. Kay and S. Bull, 'New Opportunities with Open Learner Models and Visual Learning Analytics', in *Artificial Intelligence in Education*, vol. 9112, C. Conati, N. Heffernan, A. Mitrovic, and M. F. Verdejo, Eds., in Lecture Notes in Computer Science, vol. 9112. Springer, 2015, pp. 666–669.

[9] F. Ricci, L. Rokach, and B. Shapira, Eds., *Recommender systems handbook*, Third edition. Springer, 2022.

[10] *[ISO/IEC TR 20748-1:2016] Information technology for learning, education and training — Learning analytics interoperability — Part 1: Reference model*, ISO/IEC TR 20748-1:2016, 2016.

[11] G. Siemens *et al.*, 'Open Learning Analytics: an integrated & modularized platform', SOLAR, Jul. 2011. [Online]. Available: www.solaresearch.org/publications/position-papers/

[12] M. Cooper, R. Ferguson, and A. Wolff, 'What can analytics contribute to accessibility in e-learning systems and to disabled students' learning?', in *Proceedings of the Sixth International Conference on Learning Analytics & Knowledge - LAK '16*, Edinburgh, UK: ACM, 2016, pp. 99–103.

[13] *Charter of Fundamental Rights of the European Union*, vol. C 326/391. 2016, p. 17. [Online]. Available: http://data.europa.eu/eli/treaty/char_2012/oj

[14] *Regulation (EU) 2016/679 of the European Parliament and of the Council*, vol. 02016R0679-20160504. 2016, p. 78. [Online]. Available: https://eur-lex.europa.eu/legal-content/EN/TXT/?uri=CELEX%3A02016R0679-20160504

[15] N. P. de Koch, 'Software Engineering for Adaptive Hypermedia Systems', Ludwig-Maximilians-Universität München, München, 2000.

[16] O. Abdennour, H. Kemouss, M. Erradi, and M. Khaldi, 'From Learner Profile Management to Learner Model Modeling', in *Advances in Educational Technologies and Instructional Design*, M. Khaldi, Ed., IGI Global, 2023, pp. 71–93.

[17] L. Lin and F. Wang, 'Adaptive Learning System Based on Knowledge Graph', in *International Conference on Education and Training Technologies*, in ICETT '23. New York, NY, USA: Association for Computing Machinery, 2023.

[18] L. Yang, Y. Yu, and Y. Wei, 'Data-Driven Artificial Intelligence Recommendation Mechanism in Online Learning Resources', *International Journal of Crowd Science*, vol. 6, no. 3, pp. 150–157, 2022.

[19] X. Li and S. He, 'Research and Analysis of Student Portrait Based on Campus Big Data', in *International Conference on Big Data Analytics (ICBDA)*, 2021, pp. 23–27.

[20] Y. Jun-min, X. Song, L. Da-Xiong, W. Zhi-Feng, H. Peng-Wei, and X. Chen, 'Research on the Construction and Application of Individual Learner Model', in *International Conference on Computing and Information Technology*, Procedia Computer Science, 2018, pp. 88–92.

[21] D. Hooshyar, M. Pedaste, K. Saks, Ä. Leijen, E. Bardone, and M. Wang, 'Open learner models in supporting self-regulated learning in higher education: A systematic literature review', *Computers & Education*, vol. 154, p. 103878, 2020.

[22] S. Ouf, M. A. Ellatif, S. E. Salama, and Y. Helmy, 'A proposed paradigm for smart learning environment based on semantic web', *Computers in Human Behavior*, vol. 72, pp. 796–818, 2017.

[23] X. Wang, Y. Maeda, and H.-H. Chang, 'Development and techniques in learner model in adaptive e-learning system: A systematic review', *Computers & Education*, vol. 225, p. 105184, 2025.

[24] A. Zanellati, D. D. Mitri, M. Gabbrielli, and O. Levrini, 'Hybrid Models for Knowledge Tracing: A Systematic Literature Review', *IEEE Trans. Learning Technol.*, vol. 17, pp. 1021–1036, 2024.

[25] *IEdTech Learner Information Package Specification*, Standard, Mar. 09, 2001. [Online]. Available: https://site.imsglobal.org/standards/sldm

[26] *[IEEE P1484.2] - Standard for Information Technology — Learning Systems — Learner Model*, PAR IEEE P1484.2, 1997.

[27] W. QIU, J. DU, and F. LI, 'Knowledge Description Frame of Learning Resources for Recommendation System: From the Perspectives of Learning Psychology', in *2020 15th International Conference on Computer Science & Education (ICCSE)*, 2020, pp. 438–440.

[28] X. Zhao, 'Research on learner model of adaptive learning system', in *International Conference on Computer Science & Education (ICCSE)*, 2021, pp. 906–909.

[29] S. Wang, L. Yuan, and H. Yang, 'User Model Construction of Chinese Learners Based on Learning Style', in *International Conference on Computer Science and Educational Informatization (CSEI)*, 2021, pp. 70–75.

[30] T. Fei Zhou, Y. Qing Pan, and L. R. Huang, 'Research on Personalized E-Learning Based on Decision Tree and RETE Algorithm', in *International Conference on Computer Systems, Electronics and Control (ICCSEC)*, 2017, pp. 1392–1396.

[31] A. N. Cormack, 'A Data Protection Framework for Learning Analytics', *Learning Analytics*, vol. 3, no. 1, 2016.

[32] Q. Liu and M. Khalil, 'Understanding privacy and data protection issues in learning analytics using a systematic review', *Brit J Educational Tech*, vol. 54, no. 6, pp. 1715–1747, 2023.

[33] T. Hoel and W. Chen, 'Privacy and data protection in learning analytics should be motivated by an educational maxim—towards a proposal', *Research and Practice in Technology Enhanced Learning*, vol. 13, no. 1, p. 20, 2018.

[34] M. Paludi, 'The Right to Privacy and Data Protection for High School Students in the Context of Digital Learning Models and Learning Analytics', in *Proceedings of the Doctoral Consortium of the Learning Analytics Summer Institute Europe 2024 (LASI Europe 2024 DC)*, 2018, pp. 1–10.

[35] H. Drachsler and W. Greller, 'Privacy and analytics: it's a DELICATE issue a checklist for trusted learning analytics', in *Proceedings of the Sixth International Conference on Learning Analytics & Knowledge - LAK '16*, Edinburgh, UK: ACM, 2016, pp. 89–98.

[36] J. Doveren, B. Heinemann, and U. Schroeder, 'Towards Guidelines for Data Protection and Privacy in Learning Analytics Implementation', in *Online-Labs in Education*, Nomos Verlagsgesellschaft mbH & Co. KG, 2022, pp. 45–52.

[37] F. Böck, 'Learner Models: Requirements analysis for Application in adaptive Learning Environments and

Recommendation Systems', in *2025 IEEE Digital Education and MOOCS Conference (DEMOcon)*, 2025.

[38] F. Böck, A. Deuerling, and D. Landes, 'Adaptive Learning Environment Reference Architecture for an Optimised Learning Process', in *2025 IEEE Global Engineering Education Conference (EDUCON)*, London, UK: IEEE, Apr. 2025, pp. 1–10.

[39] F. Böck, 'A Research Agenda for Learner Models for Adaptive Educational Digital Learning Environments', in *Futureproofing Engineering Education for Global Responsibility*, Springer Nature, 2025.

[40] N. Kano, N. Seraku, F. Takahashhi, and S. ichi Tsuji, 'Attractive Quality and Must-Be Quality', *Journal of the Japanese Society for Quality Control*, vol. 14, no. 2, pp. 147–156, 1984.

[41] Bundesministerium der Justiz, *Bundesdatenschutzgesetz*. 2017, p. 45. [Online]. Available: https://www.gesetze-im-internet.de/bdsg_2018/BDSG.pdf

[42] J. Kay, 'Learner know thyself: Student models to give learner control and responsibility', in *Proceedings of International Conference on Computers in Education*, 1997, pp. 17–24.

[43] V. Scholes, 'The ethics of using learning analytics to categorize students on risk', *Education Tech Research Dev*, vol. 64, no. 5, pp. 939–955, 2016.

[44] J. Dressel and H. Farid, 'The accuracy, fairness, and limits of predicting recidivism', *Sci. Adv.*, vol. 4, no. 1, p. eaao5580, 2018.

[45] N. Goltz and T. Dowdeswell, *Real world AI ethics for data scientists: practical case studies*. Boca Raton: CRC Press, Taylor & Francis Group, 2023.

[46] K. Kitto and S. Knight, 'Practical ethics for building learning analytics', *Br J Educ Technol*, vol. 50, no. 6, pp. 2855–2870, 2019.

[47] Y.-S. Tsai, C. Perrotta, and D. Gašević, 'Empowering learners with personalised learning approaches? Agency, equity and transparency in the context of learning analytics', *Assessment & Evaluation in Higher Education*, vol. 45, no. 4, pp. 554–567, 2020.

[48] S. Bull and J. Kay, 'SMILI☺: a Framework for Interfaces to Learning Data in Open Learner Models, Learning Analytics and Related Fields', *Int J Artif Intell Educ*, vol. 26, no. 1, pp. 293–331, 2016.

[49] S. Bull, B. Ginon, C. Boscolo, and M. Johnson, 'Introduction of Learning Visualisations and Metacognitive Support in a Persuadable Open Learner Model', in *International Conference on Learning Analytics and Knowledge*, in LAK '16. NY, USA: ACM, 2016, pp. 30–39.

[50] H. Ferreira, G. Oliveira, R. Araújo, F. Dorça, and R. Cattelan, 'An Open Model for Student Assessment Visualization', in *2019 IEEE 19th International Conference on Advanced Learning Technologies (ICALT)*, 2019, pp. 375–379.

[51] J. A. Ruipérez-Valiente, P. J. Muñoz-Merino, D. Leony, and C. D. Kloos, 'ALAS-KA: A learning analytics extension for better understanding the learning process in the Khan Academy platform', *Computers in Human Behavior*, vol. 47, pp. 139–148, 2015.

[52] C.-Y. Law, J. Grundy, R. Vasa, and A. Cain, 'An empirical study of user perceived usefulness and preference of open learner model visualisations', in *2016 IEEE Symposium on Visual Languages and Human-Centric Computing (VL/HCC)*, 2016, pp. 49–53.

[53] S. Bull and J. Kay, 'Open Learner Models', in *Advances in Intelligent Tutoring Systems*, vol. 308, R. Nkambou, J. Bourdeau, and R. Mizoguchi, Eds., in Studies in Computational Intelligence, vol. 308. Springer, 2010, pp. 301–322.

[54] J. Kay, K. Bartimote, K. Kitto, B. Kummerfeld, D. Liu, and P. Reimann, 'Enhancing learning by Open Learner Model (OLM) driven data design', *Computers and Education: Artificial Intelligence*, vol. 3, p. 100069, 2022.

[55] S. Bull, B. Ginon, C. Boscolo, and M. Johnson, 'Introduction of Learning Visualisations and Metacognitive Support in a Persuadable Open Learner Model', in *International Conference on Learning Analytics and Knowledge*, in LAK '16. NY, USA: ACM, 2016, pp. 30–39.

[56] *ISO/IEC 25010:2011 Systems and software engineering — Systems and software Quality Requirements and Evaluation (SQuaRE) — System and software quality models*, 35.080 Software 1, 2011.

[57] *ISO/IEC 25002:2024 Systems and software engineering — Systems and software Quality Requirements and Evaluation (SQuaRE) — Quality model overview and usage*, 35.080 Software 1, 2024.

[58] W. Kotschy, 'Art. 6 GDPR', in *The EU General Data Protection Regulation (GDPR): a commentary*, C. Kuner, C. Docksey, L. A. Bygrave, and L. Drechsler, Eds., Oxford, United Kingdom: Oxford University Press, 2019.

[59] J. T. Helmke and H. Link, 'Das Verhältnis von Art. 6 Abs. 2 und 3 DSGVO', *Datenschutz Datensich*, vol. 47, no. 11, pp. 708–714, 2023.

[60] A. Roßnagel and P. Richer, 'Art. 5', in *General data protection regulation: article-by-article commentary*, First edition., I. Spiecker Döhmann, E. Papakōnstantinu, G. Hornung, and P. de Hert, Eds., in Beck-online Bücher. , Baden-Baden, Germany: Nomos, 2023.

[61] The European Data Protection Board, 'Guidelines 01/2025 on Pseudonymisation'. Jan. 16, 2025. [Online]. Available: https://www.edpb.europa.eu/system/files/2025-01/edpb_guidelines_202501_pseudonymisation_en.pdf

[62] The European Data Protection Board, 'Guidelines 4/2019 on Article 25 Data Protection by Design and by Default, Version 2.0'. Oct. 20, 2020. [Online]. Available: https://www.edpb.europa.eu/sites/default/files/files/file1/edpb_guidelines_201904_dataprotection_by_design_and_by_default_v2.0_en.pdf

[63] Article 29 Data Protection Working Party, 'Opinion 4/2007 on the concept of personal data'. Jun. 20, 2007. [Online]. Available: https://ec.europa.eu/justice/article-29/documentation/opinion-recommendation/files/2007/wp136_en.pdf

[64] P. Schantz, 'Art. 44', in *General data protection regulation: article-by-article commentary*, First edition., I. Spiecker Döhmann, E. Papakōnstantinu, G. Hornung, and P. de Hert, Eds., in Beck-online Bücher. Baden-Baden, Germany: Nomos, 2023.

Risk-Aware HTN Planning Domain Models for Autonomous Vehicles and Satellites

Ebaa Alnazer, Ilche Georgievski, Marco Aiello
Service Computing Department, IAAS
University of Stuttgart
Stuttgart, Germany
e-mail: {ebaa.alnazer | ilche.georgievski | marco.aiello}@iaas.uni-stuttgart.de

Abstract—**The real world is characterised by uncertainty and risks. When modelling it as a domain for planning systems, this translates into action outcomes that can not be fully anticipated. In such environments, automating planning requires not only sophisticated algorithms but also domain models that adequately capture such complexity and unpredictability. However, existing AI planning domains often oversimplify these complexities, either because they are designed as benchmarks to evaluate planners or because they were created to test specific methods, frequently at the cost of broader realism. Autonomous vehicles and satellites are representative application examples that pose common planning challenges in dynamic, uncertain environments. Taking these, current domain models frequently omit critical features, such as uncertainty, risk, and the wide range of choices available to agents in achieving their objectives. Here, we contribute towards bringing these domains closer to reality by following a systematic approach to knowledge engineering and domain modelling that better captures these neglected aspects. Our models are implemented within the risk-aware Hierarchical Task Network (HTN) planning framework, which aligns with human-like reasoning and accommodates uncertainty and risk. By enhancing the realism of these two domains, our work increases their relevance for practical applications. Also, this work aims to drive the development of more capable AI planners and encourage the creation of more realistic domain models.**

Keywords-autonomous vehicles; satellites; HTN planning; knowledge engineering; domain models; risk; uncertainty

I. Introduction

Autonomous systems, such as satellites and autonomous vehicles are increasingly relied upon to perform complex tasks with minimal human intervention [1][2]. Most satellite and driving operations often take the form of complex planning problems that go beyond familiar and straightforward tasks in everyday life, where planning is typically implicit. Whether navigating dynamic traffic scenarios or coordinating satellite activities, effective planning must account for the complexities and inherent characteristics of real-world environments, such as *uncertainty*, *risk*, and the facing of a broad range of available options for achieving goals. Failing to incorporate these factors can lead to plans that are impractical, unrealistic, and often incapable of accomplishing the intended tasks.

Accounting for these complexities is equally important when automating the planning process, which is of primary concern in Artificial Intelligence (AI) planning. In its simplest form, AI planning involves generating a course of action that, when executed in a given initial state of the world, will achieve a specified user objective [3]. The set of possible actions from which the planning system constructs this course of action is derived from knowledge about the application domain. These actions are encoded in a structured, templated representation known as a *domain model*. The domain model encapsulates the relevant domain knowledge in terms of action templates with preconditions and effects, and interactions among actions. The domain model becomes even more intricate when incorporating more features, such as uncertainty, or defining different levels of abstraction, such as in the case of Hierarchical Task Network (HTN) planning [4]. As a consequence, the practical utility of AI planning is tightly coupled with the precision, completeness, and correctness of the engineered domain model, as it directly affects the AI planning system's capabilities to produce and execute valid plans [5].

Engineering adequate domain models remains one of the major barriers to the wider adoption of planning technologies [6][7]. This challenge stems from three key issues: **(1)** the lack of standard methodologies, tools, and frameworks to support the knowledge-engineering process [5][8], **(2)** the prevalence of domain models designed for benchmarking and evaluating AI planning systems, rather than real-world applicability, and **(3)** the limited focus on capturing realistic domain aspects [9]. As a consequence of **(1)**, domain models are often developed in an ad-hoc manner, heavily relying on the expertise of knowledge engineers and the tools they use [8][10]. As a consequence of **(2)**, benchmarks are oversimplified domain models with features that match the capabilities of the AI planners, e.g., the Satellite benchmark HTN domain model omits uncertainty [11]. As a consequence of **(3)**, the coverage of relevant application domains is limited, e.g., the autonomous vehicles domain remains largely unexplored in the AI planning literature.

To address these challenges, we systematically engineer and model two planning domains: Satellite and Autonomous Vehicles (AVs). In response to **(1)**, we follow a systematic approach for developing the two domain models aligned with existing knowledge-engineering processes [5][10][12], apply the conceptual framework for capturing realistic aspects in planning domains [9], and adopt the *risk-aware Hierarchical Task Network (HTN) planning framework* [13], which enables explicit modelling of risk and uncertainty through probability distributions over action costs, while leveraging the expressiveness and performance strengths of HTN planning itself. To move beyond **(2)**, we extend the benchmark Satellite domain model featured in the International Planning Competition (IPC) of 2020 by incorporating the realistic aspects of risk in terms of action costs, uncertainty, and variety of possible choices. To address **(3)**, we develop a domain model for AVs, which captures various realistic driving tasks and conditions. Lastly, we not only model both domains using a standard planning language, but also extend the Hierarchical Domain Definition Language (HDDL) [14] to allow specifying a probability distribution of action costs.

The remainder of the paper is organised as follows. Section II provides the necessary background. Section III presents the related work. Sections V and IV provide details about the knowledge engineering and modelling of the Autonomous Vehicles and Satellite domains, respectively. Section VI contains concluding remarks.

II. Background

A. Knowledge Engineering and Modelling in AI Planning

AI planning is a knowledge-based technique, meaning that to compute plans, an AI planning system requires relevant and adequate knowledge about the domain in which it is supposed to act [8][12]. Engineering and modelling such knowledge constitute the first phases of the design and development of a deployable AI planning system [12]. In the first phase, relevant requirements should be identified and defined. Having such requirements is of utmost importance as it affects the adequacy of the intended domain model and the suitability of the planning system to address the challenges of the application domain. Thus, this phase is crucial as it provides the ingredients necessary to select a suitable planning type, design a planning domain model, and design or select the planning system. The main concern of the second phase is the selection of a suitable planning type; in our case, this is risk-aware HTN planning. In the third phase, the knowledge-engineering process focuses on formulating the domain knowledge to construct a domain model [8]. The domain model is an abstract conceptual description of the application domain of interest used to represent knowledge within a planning application. This conceptual description comes from the requirement specification obtained in the first phase and covers the dynamics of the domain, the kind of problems the planning engine will have to solve, and the kind of plans (solutions) that need to be provided as output [10]. Then, an explicit formal representation or encoding is created.

The domain model formally describes the persistent knowledge and represents entities invariant over every planning problem [10][15]. These include objects with their relations and properties, actions that can change the state of the environment, and other constructs, such as tasks in HTN planning. A corresponding problem instance is needed to formally describe particular planning scenarios, which include the initial world state and the goal to be achieved. Domain models and problem instances are encoded in a de-facto standard syntax, such as HDDL and Hierarchical Planning Definition Language (HPDL) [16].

B. Realistic Aspects in Planning Domains

Accurate knowledge encoding and management in the third phase is crucial, as poor or incomplete knowledge can result in domain models that misrepresent the application domain [17], ultimately producing plans that fail in real-world execution [18]. Thus, a crucial step in the requirement analysis is the identification of relevant aspects characterising the application domain. We therefore apply an existing conceptual framework for identifying and categorising aspects of real-world planning domains, enabling the requirements analysis and aiding the knowledge-engineering process [9].

In this conceptual framework, one important aspect is the hierarchical relationship between tasks, where higher-level tasks are abstractions that can be decomposed into subtasks. The hierarchy naturally introduces structured causality, enabling reasoning across different abstraction levels. Additionally, multiple refinement options to achieve the same high-level task must be considered, where certain refinements may only be valid under specific constraints [11].

Other realistic aspects include the inherent uncertainty in real-world planning domains. It is especially important to study the sources of this uncertainty. When considering the executing agents, whether systems, humans, or a combination, uncertainty can originate internally, from the agent itself (e.g., system reliability, human limitations, irrational behaviour), or externally, from environmental factors beyond the agent's control. Both internal and external sources can be classified as either random (stochastic, rare, and unpredictable) or regular (pattern-driven and consistent).

Executing actions alters the environment and incurs costs, i.e., consumes resources, such as money, time, fuel, or effort, which are predictable in a certain world. Under uncertainty, however, action costs become variable, i.e., they are not always the same each time an action is performed. This variability stems from different sources of uncertainty: if the source is random, cost variability is unpredictable and cannot be addressed in offline planning. If the source is regular, the variability can be better defined. When cost distributions of actions are known or statistically inferable, actions are considered *risk-inducing*. When distributions instead reflect the decision maker's beliefs, the actions are *uncertainty-inducing*.

C. Risk-Aware HTN Planning

In [13], we developed risk-aware HTN planning, a framework that extends classical HTN planning with constructs that consider the uncertainty of real-world environments. It enables modelling of risk- and uncertainty-inducing actions through probability distributions over their costs and effects, where costs are defined as unbounded negative functions. The framework can be tailored for planning problems where actions have deterministic effects but variable costs. In our domain models, we adopt this variation as an initial step toward incorporating risk and uncertainty into HTN planning domain models.

The cost functions of actions can be of different types depending on the factors/sources of the costs. The cost function can be (1) *external* ($c^{ie}(a)$), i.e., it depends on external factors not explicitly modelled in the domain, such as market electricity prices or taxes, (2) *state-dependent* ($c^{is}(a)$), i.e., it is based on the system's current state, like the vehicle's charging level or position, (3) *constant* ($c^{ic}(a)$), i.e., it remains the same for every execution of an action, such as a fixed charging price, or (4) external and state-dependent, i.e., a *hybrid function* ($c^{ies}(a)$), which depends on both current state and external factors, where a denotes an action.

III. Related Work

Existing Satellite and AVs domains exhibit the discussed issues, that is, the limited realism. A version of the Satellite domain is modelled for the HTN planning track in the IPC 2020 [19], which, unfortunately, like most benchmark domains, tends to oversimplify several real-world aspects, such as risk and uncertainty, to enable planners to find valid solutions and evaluate their performance. In our proposed model, we build on this version by analysing sources of uncertainty and their effects on action costs, allowing us to incorporate risk. We also expand the range of tasks and increase the number of alternative methods for completing space missions. In our previous work, we focused particularly on extending the Satellite domain by providing alternatives for how captured images of spatial phenomena are sent to Earth, but did not consider uncertainty and risk [11]. In [20], the authors model a Satellite domain for onboard and online planning using a language based on an extended HTN representation. While their model captures several real-world aspects, such as unexpected events and resource consumption, it does not incorporate risk modelling, as planning is assumed to occur online. Another line of work on the Satellite domain focuses on modelling TV and communication satellites (e.g., [21]), which is semantically different from the space exploration satellite domain we propose.

Existing works that model the domain of autonomous vehicles for AI planning are rather scarce. In [11], we model an HTN planning domain for autonomous vehicles, taking into account various autonomous driving tasks, but do not consider realistic aspects such as uncertainty and risk. Several studies have explored traffic control problems in classical planning and extensions of it, focusing on automating multi-vehicle navigation to manage traffic [22]–[26]. Route planning research in AI planning is also relevant to the AV domain, with many works addressing marine environments and incorporating uncertainty (e.g., [27]). Although autonomous underwater vehicles share some route planning tasks with autonomous vehicles, their environments and other tasks differ significantly. Other works address route planning within a temporal HTN planning framework in the aerial domain (e.g., [28]), focusing on challenges that are distinct from those faced in autonomous ground vehicle contexts.

IV. Satellite

The Satellite domain involves space applications with autonomous orbiting spacecraft that perform tasks such as imaging, data collection, navigation, or scientific research. The domain we extend originates from the partial-order track of the IPC-2020 benchmark for HTN planning, based on a NASA application where satellites conduct stellar observations by capturing images of spatial phenomena [19].

We chose this domain because it exemplifies real-world complexities and challenges for planning, including multiple satellite missions under strict resource constraints, namely, limited power, restricted target access, constrained time windows for downlinking data to ground stations, and high operational costs [29][30].

A. Relevant Real-World Aspects

Following the vision presented in [11], the original domain is enhanced. We begin by identifying and gathering relevant aspects using the conceptual framework we proposed in [9], with particular emphasis on unaddressed factors in the original domain, such as additional stellar observation tasks and their associated complexities and interdependencies; sources of uncertainty; domain-specific quantities such as resources and variable action costs; and the objectives pursued by autonomous satellites.

Satellites perform multiple tasks to make stellar observations. These tasks are of multiple abstraction levels and have structured causality, where complex tasks are achieved by performing multiple subtasks [9]. Basically, the satellites are equipped with several observation instruments, each of which has specific modes like infrared, spectrograph, X-ray, and thermography, and has defined calibration targets (directions). Performing a space mission is a complex task that involves preparing a satellite and then taking an image. Preparing the satellite requires routing energy to an instrument, properly calibrating the instrument, and turning the satellite in the direction of the phenomenon to be captured. Finally, the satellite can capture an image of the targeted phenomenon. In actual operations, it is often necessary to activate multiple instruments simultaneously due to limitations in time and resources [31]. Therefore, the satellite must be capable of powering on several instruments at once and should be able to choose how many instruments to activate, taking into account, for example, the possibility of power failure.

Satellite mission complexity arises from the inherent uncertainty of space environments and the technologies used for the satellite operations and its instruments. Planning stellar observations requires accounting for uncertainties and their inherent randomness—specifically, what is known during the planning phase versus what becomes known only at execution time. Key sources of uncertainty, and their impact on resource consumption (e.g., time and power) include: (1) *Internal sources*, such as limitations of physical sensors that affect data quality (e.g., resolution, accuracy, noise), introducing uncertainty into action costs when these are tied to data quality [32]. Other internal uncertainties arise from the potential for power system failures (e.g., battery or solar array malfunctions [33]), which can result in power loss during the execution of actions like powering multiple instruments on the same satellite platform [34], ultimately increasing execution time. (2) *External sources* stem from the satellite's environment. Space weather events can induce anomalies such as temporary outages, power failures, and solar cell degradation [35]. Additionally, solar energetic particles or protons can penetrate satellite electronics and cause electrical failures [36].

The satellite's goal is to perform stellar observations that optimise factors like mission time and power consumption, while considering several aspects (e.g., risk and uncertainty), and the satellite and its instruments' states.

B. Domain Model Formulation

Next, we formulate the gathered knowledge as a prerequisite to model the Satellite domain.

1) Stellar Observation Tasks – Complexities and Relations: Knowledge about stellar observation tasks is represented as compound and primitive tasks. Compound tasks capture abstraction levels, causality, recursion, conditions, and alternatives, and can be decomposed by various methods into subtasks.

An abstract (or general) graphical overview of this HTN domain model is shown in Figure 1, where blue nodes represent compound tasks, orange nodes represent primitive tasks, and grey nodes $v_{m_0}, v_{m_1}, \ldots, v_{m_{11}}$ represent methods. Nodes encircled by green are our extensions. The domain includes a single top-level task, `do_observation`, which achieves a stellar observation mission by preparing the instrument and taking an image. This task can be decomposed using four methods, v_{m_0} to v_{m_3}, which represent different situational contexts rather than alternative strategies of performing the observation task. Their main differences lie in the preparation phase. Specifically, v_{m_0} includes `activate_instrument`, `turn_to`, and `take_image`; v_{m_1} omits instrument activation, assuming it is pre-calibrated, possibly from previous observations; v_{m_2} skips turning; and v_{m_3} performs only `take_image`.

Each satellite can have multiple instruments onboard. In the original domain, only one instrument can be powered per satellite. This is governed by switching off any active instrument before powering on another, and making the power unavailable after switching on an instrument. This behaviour is modelled through the methods v_{m_4} and v_{m_7}. v_{m_4} decomposes `activate_instrument` into `switch_off`, `switch_on` to switch off an already powered instrument and switch on the instrument corresponding to the required mode, respectively, and `auto_calibrate`. The latter is further decomposed by $v_{m_{10}}$ and $v_{m_{11}}$, where $v_{m_{10}}$ decomposes the task into `turn_to` to slew the satellite into the calibration direction and `calibrate` to calibrate the instrument, while $v_{m_{11}}$ skips turning, assuming the satellite is already aligned. v_{m_7} is applicable when there is no powered-on instrument, thus it skips switching off.

Real-world satellite missions often require activating multiple instruments simultaneously due to time and resource constraints [31], a capability missing from the original domain. This calls for additional methods for the `activate_instrument` task, allowing satellites to power multiple instruments concurrently and incorporating permissive decomposition into the domain model.

Powering several instruments in parallel risks power failure/loss if the satellite's energy source (e.g., solar panels, Radioisotope Thermoelectric Generators, or helium cells)

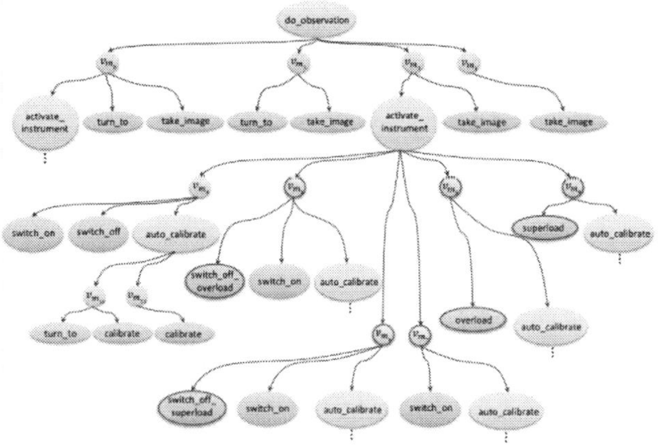

Figure 1. HTN model for the Satellite domain.

cannot meet demand [34], potentially causing delays to recover. To model this, we add methods v_{m_8}, v_{m_9}, v_{m_5}, and v_{m_6}. v_{m_8} and v_{m_9} decompose the task into `overload` or `superload` (to switch on second or third instruments), followed by `auto_calibrate`. v_{m_5} and v_{m_6} decompose the task into `switch_off_overload` or `switch_off_superload` to switch off two or three instruments at once, respectively, followed by `switch_on` and `auto_calibrate`. Thus, v_{m_4} and v_{m_8} are alternatives: to power a second instrument, the planner can either switch off the first or overload the satellite. Likewise, v_{m_5} and v_{m_9} offer a choice between switching off two instruments or adding a third, resulting in a "superload" with three active instruments.

2) Non-determinism and Action Costs: To model non-determinism and action costs, we analyse how internal and external uncertainty sources affect actions that rely on a stable satellite power system. We focus on the cost variability of `overload` and `superload`, which place higher demands on power. Specifically, considering that costs are indicative of the time required for actions to be completed, activating a second instrument via the `overload` action has a 99% probability of taking 15 units of time and a 1% probability of taking 100 units of time due to power failure. `superload` is riskier as the unfavourable outcome incurs more often and has a higher likelihood of occurrence, with a 95% probability of taking 15 units of time and a 5% probability of taking 400 units of time. All other actions are assigned a fixed cost of 15 units with 100% probability, enabling a clear comparison of planner behaviour under different risk attitudes concerning the simultaneous or sequential activation and deactivation of instruments. Here, we use the constant cost function type $c^{ic}(a)$. This means that the action costs are defined within the domain model and remain consistent across different problem instances. However, other types of cost functions and alternative cost distributions can also be considered, as the statistical inferences used to derive them may vary across different satellite domains.

3) Planning Problems Instances: Knowledge about planning problems is formulated so that the initial state contains the knowledge about the static and dynamic environment states.

The static state includes each satellite's instrument, supported modes, and the calibration target of each instrument. The dynamic state includes the available power and current pointing direction of individual satellites. The initial task network includes all required observation missions, each targeting a phenomenon with a specified mode.

C. Domain Model Encoding

We model the planning knowledge formulated earlier directly into risk-aware HTN planning constructs. Listing 1 shows part of the domain model, including the `switch_on`, `overload`, and `superload` actions. `switch_on` is executed when the satellite's power is available and makes it unavailable. In contrast, `overload` and `superload` can be executed when the power is unavailable, but introduce a risk of power failure. That is, we assume that the `(power_avail)` predicate represents a restriction of maximum power for safety purposes that can be ignored when choosing to overload or superload the satellite. Recovery time from failure is modelled using probabilistic cost distributions via the : $costdist$ construct, followed by the probability distribution in the form of $(or(p_1(c_1)(p_2(c_2))\dots(p_n(c_n))$.

Listing 1: Switch on, overload, and superload actions in the Satellite domain.

```
(:action switch_on
 :parameters (?so_i - instrument ?so_s - satellite)
 :precondition (and (on_board ?so_i ?so_s)(power_avail ?
     so_s))
 :effect (and (power_on ?so_i)(not(calibrated ?so_i))(not(
     power_avail ?so_s)))
 :costdist (or (1(15))))

(:action overload
 :parameters (?so_i - instrument ?so_s - satellite)
 :precondition (and (on_board ?so_i ?so_s)(not(overloaded ?
     so_s))(not(power_avail ?so_s)))
 :effect (and (power_on ?so_i)(overloaded ?so_s)(overloads
     ?so_i ?so_s)(not(calibrated ?so_i)))
 :costdist (or (0.99(15)) (0.01(100))))

(:action superload
 :parameters (?so_i - instrument ?so_s - satellite)
 :precondition (and (on_board ?so_i ?so_s)(overloaded ?so_s
     )(not(power_avail ?so_s))(not(superloaded ?so_s)))
 :effect (and (power_on ?so_i)(superloaded ?so_s)(
     superloads ?so_i ?so_s)(not(calibrated ?so_i)))
 :costdist (or (0.95(15)) (0.05(400))))
```

V. AUTONOMOUS VEHICLES

Autonomous vehicles are transportation means, typically for humans or working under human delegation, that can navigate without or with little human direct control. We choose this application domain as it exhibits realistic characteristics commonly found in real-world scenarios, many of which present significant challenges for both the modelling and solving of planning problems. These challenges originate from the domain's inherent complexity and uncertainty, such as road incidents and varying road conditions, risk factors, diverse driving tasks, resource constraints like travel time and fuel or charge levels, and the critical need to track the vehicle's state and its environment.

A. Relevant Real-world Aspects

We start by covering the aspects of driving tasks and their complexities and relations, the non-determinism in the domain, including the sources of uncertainty and their randomness, quantities in this domain, including resources and action costs and the variability of action costs as a consequence of non-determinism, and the objectives of an autonomous vehicle.

An autonomous vehicle performs various driving tasks to navigate routes and reach required destinations successfully. These driving tasks are of multiple abstraction levels and have structured causality, where complex tasks are achieved by performing multiple subtasks, such as route planning, navigation, and vehicle control [9]. For example, reaching a destination may require moving between intermediate locations, stopping, starting the engine, and managing turn signals. The vehicle must also handle road contingencies (e.g., pedestrians, construction), which consist of subtasks like stopping, dodging the incident, or restarting the engine. Environmental factors such as slippery roads introduce further complexity, requiring actions like activating the Electronic Stability Program (ESP) and adjusting speed. As in many real-world domains, these tasks can be achieved in various ways. For example, a vehicle might address poor road conditions by decelerating or accelerating with or without activating the ESP, and it may choose from various routes to reach a destination.

The complexity of AV driving tasks arises mainly from the dynamic and uncertain environment common to real-world domains [9]. Planning these tasks must account for uncertainty sources and their randomness, i.e., the amount of knowledge that can be defined when planning the driving tasks. Following our previous work [9][13], we categorise uncertainty sources based on the vehicle's autonomy level: (1) non-autonomous (human-driven), (2) fully autonomous (no human intervention), and (3) semi-autonomous (shared control). These uncertainties may be internal, originating from the agent performing the tasks, or external, from the environment. (1) For human drivers, internal regular uncertainties often relate to variations in driving skills, habits, intentions, tactics, and speed. For instance, travel time and energy consumption can vary depending on a driver's speed preferences, habits, and tactics. Additionally, fatigue may lead to accidents, such as falling asleep at the wheel. The consequences caused by driver drowsiness have been statistically studied [37]. Unlike regular sources that can be statistically anticipated, some internal sources are random and rare, such as a driver having a stroke, making them difficult to predict. (2) For fully autonomous systems, internal regular uncertainties may result from control variability, such as the vehicle's ability to stabilise on a slippery road, leading to variable driving times and consumed energy. There are also some random internal sources that lead to unpredictable outcomes. For example, a flat tire will cause the car to stop. (3) Finally, semi-autonomous vehicles inherit a mix of these uncertainties, as both the human driver and the autonomous system contribute to the vehicle's operation.

External sources of uncertainty, both regular and random,

can also affect cost variability. For example, a vehicle may fail to charge due to an unexpected station malfunction or encounter an unplanned roadblock from an accident. Such rare events are difficult to predict during planning, making action outcomes uncertain. Now consider external sources of uncertainty that are regular, such as weather conditions. Weather conditions, for instance, change constantly and cannot be predicted with full certainty. Due to the chaotic nature of the atmosphere and limitations in observation and modelling, forecasts inherently include uncertainty [38]. To express this, weather is often reported using probabilistic forecasts, where elements like temperature, wind, and precipitation are probabilistically quantified [39]. Another regular external source of uncertainty is traffic, which significantly impacts action cost variability. For example, when planning a route with Google Maps, the most used route planning application, estimated travel times for the same route vary due to regular factors like traffic. As shown in Figure 2, there is an estimation of the travelling time, i.e., a range of potential travelling times, for each route the vehicle can take, and these estimates differ between weekdays and weekends, with shorter times typically observed on weekends due to lighter traffic. Similarly, queues at charging stations represent another regular external uncertainty. To improve the quality of service at charging stations, studies such as [40] predict the probability of waiting times, which directly affect charging duration and overall trip time.

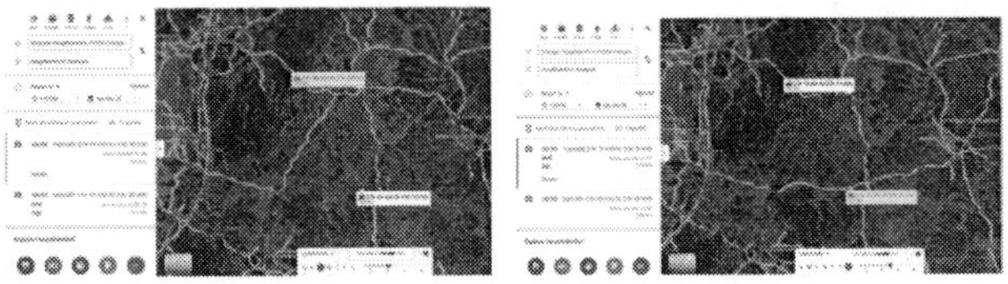

(a) Travelling times on a workday [41]. (b) Travelling times on a weekend [42].

Figure 2. Variability of travelling times in Google Maps.

In addition to the factors discussed, it is crucial to account for resource consumption, i.e., action costs such as time, money, energy, effort, or even human lives, which is a common concern in real-world domains [9]. The presence of uncertainty makes these costs variable. Therefore, understanding and modelling cost variability is essential for effective planning. For instance, uncertainty in weather forecasts affects driving costs; travelling between two locations in winter may require more time and energy if it is snowing. How much knowledge we have about the probability distribution of action costs depends on how much knowledge we have about the uncertainty sources. When uncertainty is represented probabilistically, such as through weather forecasts, associated delays can also be estimated probabilistically, a concept known as risk (see Section II-B). Conversely, random uncertainty sources like unpredictable accidents lead to costs, e.g., delays, injuries, financial loss, and environmental impact, that are difficult to quantify probabilistically. Such events can reduce road capacity, increase congestion and travel time, and potentially cause further incidents [43].

Given the above knowledge, the goal of the autonomous driving task is to find routes that optimise some objective (e.g., commuting time) while considering several aspects (e.g., risk, uncertainty, and alternative choices on how to achieve tasks), the vehicle's general state (e.g., current location), the states of its components (e.g., headlights), and the various environmental factors (e.g., weather and road conditions) to promote better safety and user experience.

B. Domain Model Formulation

1) Driving Tasks – Complexities and Relations: Tasks are formulated as compound and primitive tasks, where the relation between these tasks, i.e., the abstraction levels, structured causality, recursion, conditions, and alternatives, is formulated as hierarchical levels, where compound tasks can be decomposed by various methods, which represent the ways to achieve these tasks, into subtasks (compound and primitive). Thus, we can model the various driving tasks performed by the AV to navigate routes and reach required destinations successfully as HTN tasks, forming the HTN domain model for the AV domain. An abstract (or general) graphical overview of this HTN domain model is shown in Figure 3. The domain has one task, `drive`, at the highest level of the hierarchy, which enables travel between two locations. Three different methods can decompose this task, denoted as v_{m_1}, v_{m_2}, and v_{m_3}. The first method v_{m_1} is applicable when the vehicle does not have enough power to travel to the next location. To recharge, the vehicle must drive to a charging station (`drive`), recharge (`recharge`), and from there to its original destination (`drive`). The second method v_{m_2} is applicable when the vehicle is charged and has not reached its destination. In this case, the vehicle's engine should be cranked if it was not before (`start`), the lights are turned on if they were off and it is nighttime (`turnon`), and the vehicle moves one step to the next location (`move_step`). Then, the `drive` task is recursively decomposed again to move the vehicle to the next intermediate location until reaching the destination. The third method v_{m_3} becomes applicable if the vehicle is at the destination. This method decomposes the `drive` task to a single compound task `stop_vehilce` to stop the vehicle, which in turn is decomposed by two methods v_{m_4} and v_{m_5}. The former decomposes the task into a single primitive task to stop the engine. The latter is applicable when the engine is already off, and it decomposes the `stop_vehicle` into an empty task network, symbolised by the `nop` primitive task. These methods implement a form of phantomisation that can be encountered in HTNs [44].

The `move_step` compound task is decomposed by two different methods v_m_{10} and v_m_{11}, based on whether the road is free from any complexity or not, respectively. In the first case, the `move_step` task is decomposed by $v_{m_{10}}$ into a single primitive task `accelerate`. In the second case, the task is decomposed by $v_{m_{11}}$ into two consecutive compound tasks `handle_incidents` and `handle_road_conditions`. The `handle_incidents` task can be decomposed by two

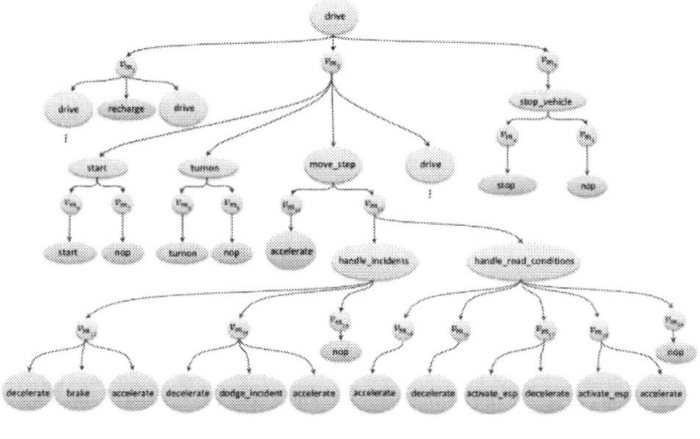

Figure 3. HTN model for the domain of Autonomous Vehicles. Blue nodes represent compound tasks, orange nodes represent primitive tasks, and grey nodes $v_{m_1}, v_{m_2}, \ldots, v_{m_{19}}$ represent methods.

different methods $v_{m_{13}}$ and $v_{m_{12}}$, based on whether the incident is still (e.g., rocks and construction work), or moving (e.g., pedestrians crossing the street). In the first case, the vehicle must decelerate, dodge the incident, and then accelerate again. In the second case, the vehicle should decelerate, brake to allow the moving incident to cross the road, and accelerate again. The `handle_road_conditions` task can be decomposed by four different methods $v_{m_{15}}$, $v_{m_{16}}$, $v_{m_{17}}$ and $v_{m_{18}}$. All these four methods are applicable when the road is, for example, icy, slippery, under construction, or has loose gravel, and they result in accelerating without caring about the road condition, only decelerating, activating the ESP and decelerating, activating the ESP but accelerating, respectively. These methods have the same preconditions which relate to road conditions being abnormal. This makes all four methods applicable at the same time during planning, and the planning agent always has the choice between these methods. We refer to this concept as *permissive decomposition* or *non-exclusive decomposition*. Note that both the `handle_incidents` and `handle_road_conditions` have an additional method each ($v_{m_{14}}$ and $v_{m_{19}}$) that decomposes the corresponding tasks into an empty task network when there are no incidents or road conditions, respectively. These methods constitute another form of phantomisation [44]. This modelling choice allows us to handle situations where there are road conditions and incidents at the same time between two connected locations.

2) Non-determinism: Uncertainty Sources and their Randomness: Here, we formulate the knowledge related to the non-determinism of the domain and the quantities. While we do not explicitly formulate the knowledge related to the various uncertainty sources encountered in the AV domain, we formulate the direct effects they have on the cost of driving actions performed in this domain, making them variable. In this domain model, we consider the effects of three sources of uncertainty, namely (1) the speed at which the pedestrians walk the pedestrian crossing, which is considered a regular external source of uncertainty, (2) the traffic on roads, which is also considered an external regular source of uncertainty, and (3) the ability of the autonomous vehicle to stabilise on slippery roads, which is considered an internal regular source of uncertainty.

3) Quantities: Resources and Action Costs: When this variability of costs comes from regular uncertainty sources, such as traffic jams, it can be described by a probability distribution that can be either known or statistically inferred (see Section II-B). Actions here are risk-inducing. In the present treatment, we define driving costs as the time needed to drive through the roads and deal with the various road complexities. That is, the existence of uncertain traffic jams during planning makes the estimation of travelling times variable (as shown in Figure 2). While we use risk-inducing actions and travelling times as costs to exemplify a possible formulation of the domain knowledge, uncertainty-inducing actions and other types of costs, such as fuel/power consumption, comfort of the ride, and road windingness, could be used.

Since in the AVs domain, the travelling costs can depend on the traffic jams and on the particular road itself, e.g., its length and conditions, we use a hybrid, external and state-dependent cost function $c^{ies}(a)$ to compute the costs (see Section II-C). In particular, the estimation of uncertain traffic jams comes from an external function, and each road's length and other properties represent a state-dependent cost function that is defined with respect to the ground planning problem. These two functions can be combined into one hybrid function that computes the probability distribution of travelling times.

4) Planning Problems Instances: Knowledge about planning problems is formulated such that the initial state contains the knowledge about the static and the dynamic states of the environment. The static state includes the road network, i.e., locations and routes connecting them, the location of still and moving incidents (e.g., construction works and pedestrians), the conditions of roads (e.g., slippery roads, roads with gravel, and normal roads), and the length of the roads. The dynamic states include the location of the vehicle. The initial task network in the planning problem is to move the vehicle from one location to another. The objects are the locations that the vehicle can navigate to and the various incidents.

5) Example of a Problem Instance: Let us consider an example of a planning problem with seven different locations denoted as S, l_1, l_2, l_3, l_4, l_5, and E, depicted in Figure 4. The vehicle is initially at S and should navigate to E while handling the various road complexities. We assume that the vehicle has enough power to navigate all the roads, and it is nighttime, so the vehicle has to turn on the lights. The roads between S and l_1 and between S and l_3 are complexity-free. However, the first road is longer than the second. The road between l_1 and l_4 has constructions at location l_2. The road between l_3 and l_4 has a school area that is very crowded with pedestrians and traffic jams, i.e., moving incidents, at location l_5. The road between l_1 and l_3 is a highway free from any complexities, but has a variable level of traffic congestion. Finally, the road between l_4 and E is icy and slippery.

Figure 5 shows some possible bindings of the actions with the corresponding probability distribution of costs with respect to the ground planning problem and external traffic as sources

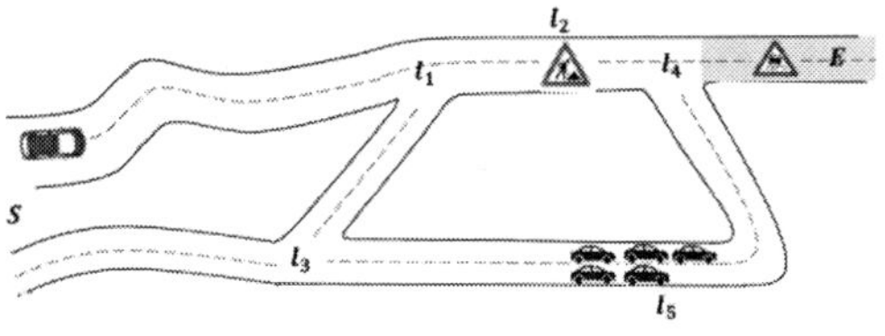

Figure 4. A problem instance in the AVs domain with seven locations S, l_1, l_2, l_3, l_4, l_5, and E, and various road complexities.

of uncertainty. Note that we only show feasible bindings and ground actions that can be part of the computed plans. For example, the action of accelerating has a probability distribution of costs when the vehicle is accelerating on the road between S and l_1, different from the probability distribution of costs when accelerating on the road between S and l_3, since the length and traffic jams of these roads are different. The logic behind our assignments of the action variable costs is as follows. The road between S and l_1 is complexity-free and free of traffic jams. Thus, the time needed to drive through this road is certain, i.e., driving through this road takes four hours with 100% probability. On the other hand, although shorter, the road between S and l_3 has a variable traffic jam throughout the day. Driving through this road can take six hours with 20% probability, or two hours, in the best case, with 80% probability. Thus, taking the short road is riskier than taking the long road. The road between l_1 and l_4 has construction work at location l_2. Since the construction is considered a still incident, passing through this road, i.e., decelerating, dodging the constructions, and accelerating again, is done in a certain time under the assumption that this road does not include any traffic jam. In particular, cumulative deceleration on the road between l_1 and l_2 requires four hours, dodging the incident requires 0.4 hours, and accelerating on the road between l_2 and l_4 takes one hour. Unlike the road between l_1 and l_4, the road between l_3 and l_4 has multiple schools and heavy traffic at location l_5, which can lead to long waiting times. This is an external source of uncertainty since pedestrians have uncertain times and speeds at which they cross the road, which can make this area congested. Additionally, the roads between l_3 and l_5, and l_5 and l_4 have an uncertain level of traffic congestion. Thus, driving from l_3 to l_4, i.e., decelerating, braking, and accelerating, requires a variable amount of time, as shown in Figure 5. In particular, decelerating on the road between l_3 and l_5 takes one hour with 10% probability and three hours with 90% probability. Consider the school area is very crowded, and the vehicle might need to brake for a long time, waiting for the pedestrians to walk. Thus, braking before this area can take half an hour with a high probability of 90% and can, in the worst case, take three hours with a probability of 10%.

The road between l_1 and l_3 is a highway that is complexity-free. However, it has an uncertain level of traffic congestion. Thus, although the vehicle can accelerate on this road, with a small probability of 10%, it can take eight hours to reach l_3 when there is a high traffic congestion. With a high probability of 90%, the vehicle can travel from l_1 to l_3 within two hours since the highway is mostly free of traffic jams. Lastly, the road between l_4 and E is icy and slippery. If the agent chooses to decelerate without activating the ESP, the time needed to reach E will be variable and is based on the ability of the vehicle to stabilise on this slippery road. This choice can lead to six hours of driving with 20% probability and eleven hours of driving with 80% probability. If the agent chooses to decelerate after activating the ESP, it will need 10 hours, i.e., a known and certain amount of time, to reach E since this is the safest and most guaranteed option to choose. However, suppose the agent accelerates after activating the ESP. In that case, it will need an uncertain amount of time, depending on the vehicle's stability. This option is very risky since it might require 12 hours in the worst case with an 80% probability as the vehicle will probably lose stability. At the same time, there is a 20% probability that the vehicle will have good stability and reach its destination in two hours since it is accelerating. An even riskier option is to accelerate on this road without activating the ESP. In that case, the vehicle might need sixteen hours to reach location E with a probability of 90%, and, in the best case, it needs half an hour with a probability of 10%. Comparing the option of decelerating after activating the ESP with the option of decelerating without activating the ESP, the first option has a more guaranteed outcome, i.e., execution time, although both options have the same expected value, which is 10 hours. We can also see that the option of accelerating after activating the ESP is riskier than decelerating without activating the ESP, since, with an 80% probability, it might lead to a higher time than the outcome of only decelerating. Lastly, when comparing the options of decelerating without activating the ESP and only decelerating, we see that both options involve risk. However, unless the agent is highly risk-seeking, it is less likely that the first option is preferable since it has the probability of 20% of costing six hours compared to the second option, which has the probability of costing four hours less with the same 20% probability. At the same time, the first option has an 80% probability of costing eleven hours compared to twelve hours for the second option, with the same probability, which means a one-hour difference only. Note that, despite the differences in the risk level, all three options have the same expected value, which is ten hours. The only option that has a higher expected travelling time compared to all other options is accelerating without activating the ESP. That is why this option is the riskiest one and is only chosen if the agent is extremely risk-seeking. Additionally, we extend the possible roads that the vehicle can take by adding the possibility of taking a shortcut road that has a 90% probability of taking two hours and a 10% probability of taking eight hours. This extension increases the number of choices the agent should make according to its risk attitude, since taking the shortcut road can have a high risk of incurring long travelling times compared to taking several longer roads.

C. Domain Model Encoding

We encode the domain and problem instances using our extension of HDDL [14]. Compound tasks are modelled by

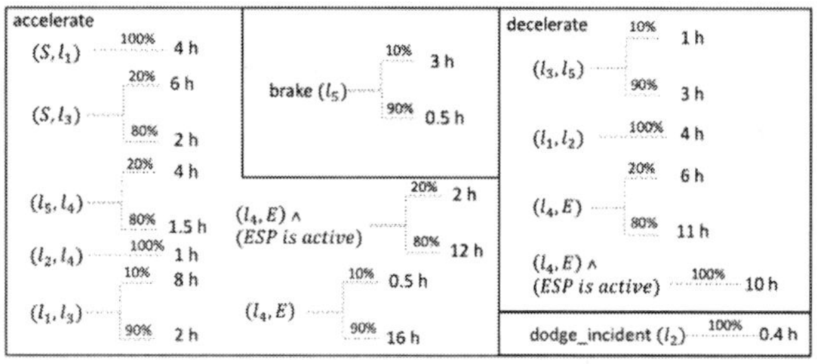

Figure 5. Actions with the corresponding possible bindings and probability distribution of costs (time).

providing the name of the task with the parameter list, as shown in Listing 2 for the `handle_incidents` compound task. Methods are modelled by providing the parameter list, the corresponding compound task, preconditions, and task network. For example, the `handle_incidents` compound task can be decomposed by three methods, where the first two are based on whether the incident is still or moving, which is ensured in the preconditions, and the third method constitutes a form of phantomisation.

Listing 2: Methods for handling incidents in the AVs domain model

```
(:method handle_incidents_0
 :parameters(?v - vehicle ?l1 ?l2 ?l3 - loc ?movinc -
    movingobs)
 :task(handle_incidents ?v ?l1 ?l2)
 :precondition(and (connected ?l1 ?l3)(connected ?l3 ?l2)(
    in-inc ?movinc ?l3))
 :ordered-subtasks(and (decelerate_incident ?v ?l1 ?l3)(
    brake ?v ?l3)(accelerate_incident ?v ?l3 ?l2)))

(:method handle_incidents_1
 :parameters(?v - vehicle ?l1 ?l2 ?l3 - loc ?stillinc -
    stillobs)
 :task(handle_incidents ?v ?l1 ?l2)
 :precondition(and(connected ?l1 ?l3)(connected ?l3 ?l2)(
    in-inc ?stillinc ?l3))
 :ordered-subtasks(and(decelerate_still_incident ?v ?l1 ?l3
    )(dodge_incident ?v ?l3 ?l2)(accelerate_still_incident
    ?v ?l3 ?l2)))

(:method handle_incidents_2
 :parameters(?v - vehicle ?l1 ?l2 - loc)
 :task(handle_incidents ?v ?l1 ?l2)
 :precondition(clearroad ?l1 ?l2)
 :ordered-subtasks())
```

Actions are modelled, as in HDDL, with a parameter list, preconditions, and effects, where risk is modelled via the construct `:costdist`. Listing 3 shows four decelerating and accelerating actions that can be performed to handle bad road conditions, each with cost distributions shown in Figure 5. Since the cost functions in this domain are hybrid, we preprocess these actions by expanding them into multiple variants based on road conditions, and directly assign the corresponding hybrid cost functions within the domain model.

Listing 3: Accelerating and decelerating actions of the AVs domain model that deal with bad road conditions.

```
(:action accelerate_bad_road
  :parameters (?v - vehicle ?l1 ?l2 - loc)
  :precondition (and (not (in ?v ?l2))(not(activated_esp ?v
    )))
  :effect (and (in ?v ?l2)(highspeed ?v))
  :costdist (or (0.9(16)) (0.1(0.5))))

(:action accelerate_after_esp
  :parameters (?v - vehicle ?l1 ?l2 - loc)
  :precondition (and (not(in ?v ?l2))(activated_esp ?v))
  :effect (and (in ?v ?l2)(highspeed ?v))
  :costdist (or (0.8(12)) (0.2(2))))

(:action decelerate_after_esp
  :parameters (?v - vehicle ?l1 ?l2 - loc)
  :precondition (and (not(in ?v ?l2))(activated_esp ?v))
  :effect (and (in ?v ?l2) (not(highspeed ?v)))
  :costdist (or (1(10))))

(:action decelerate_bad_road
  :parameters (?v - vehicle ?l1 ?l2 - loc)
  :precondition (and (not(in ?v ?l2))(not(activated_esp ?v)
   ))
  :effect (and (in ?v ?l2)(not(highspeed ?v)))
  :costdist (or (0.2(6)) (0.8(11))))
```

We model the objects existing in the planning problem, the initial task network is to drive to a destination, and the initial state is a list of predicates. Listing 4 shows the initial state of the problem instance illustrated in Figure 4.

Listing 4: Initial state of the problem instance illustrated in Figure 5.

```
(:init (connected s l1)(connected s l3)(connected l1 l4)(
    connected l3 l4)(connected l4 e)(connected l1 l2)(
    connected l2 l4)(connected l3 l5) (connected l5 l4)(
    clearroadlong s l1)(clearroad s l1)(clearroadshort s l3
    )(clearroad s l3)(in-inc construction l2)(in-inc
    bottleneck l5)(clearroad l4 e)(badroad l4 e)(in v0 s))
```

VI. Conclusions

Generating valid, capable, and executable plans for real-world scenarios requires domain models that accurately reflect the complexities of the target environments. We showed how to systematically engineer domain knowledge and model two representative domains, Satellite and Autonomous Vehicles, that embody common planning challenges in complex and dynamic environments. For the Satellite domain, we build upon existing models by explicitly incorporating elements of risk and uncertainty, and by expanding the set of methods available to achieve tasks. For the AV domain, we address a notable gap in the literature, namely, the fact that many existing works focus on traffic-level control or underwater vehicles, while few address the planning needs of individual AVs. Our approach and model fill this gap by capturing realistic driving tasks alongside key aspects such as uncertainty, risk, and the wide range of methods for tasks. Together, these contributions not only enrich the Satellite and AV domains but also provide a concrete path toward making AI planning more applicable to real-world deployment. By showing how realistic aspects can be systematically identified, incorporated, and formalised, our work lays the foundation for improving other domains and advancing planners that can operate effectively under real-world conditions.

References

[1] S. Kolski, D. Ferguson, M. Bellino, and R. Siegwart, "Autonomous Driving in Structured and Unstructured Environments", in *IV Symposium*, IEEE, 2006, pp. 558–563.

[2] D. Omeiza, H. Webb, M. Jirotka, and L. Kunze, "Explanations in Autonomous Driving: A Survey", *T-ITS*, vol. 23, no. 8, pp. 10 142–10 162, 2021.

[3] M. Ghallab, D. Nau, and P. Traverso, *Automated Planning: Theory and Practice*. Elsevier, 2004.

[4] I. Georgievski and M. Aiello, "HTN planning: Overview, comparison, and beyond", *Artificial Intelligence Journal*, vol. 222, pp. 124–156, 2015.

[5] I. Georgievski, "Software Development Life Cycle for Engineering AI Planning Systems", in *ICSOFT*, SciTePress, 2023, pp. 751–760.

[6] T. L. McCluskey, "Object Transition Sequences: A New Form of Abstraction for HTN Planners", in *AIPS*, AAAI Press, 2000, pp. 216–225.

[7] I. Georgievski, "Engineering AI Planning Systems", Habilitation Thesis, University of Stuttgart, 2025.

[8] T. L. McCluskey, T. S. Vaquero, and M. Vallati, "Engineering Knowledge for Automated Planning: Towards a Notion of Quality", in *K-CAP*, Association for Computing Machinery, 2017, pp. 1–8.

[9] E. Alnazer and I. Georgievski, "Understanding Real-World AI Planning Domains: A Conceptual Framework", in *SummerSoC*, Springer, 2023, pp. 3–23.

[10] M. Vallati and L. McCluskey, "A Quality Framework for Automated Planning Knowledge Models", in *ICAART*, SciTePress, 2021, pp. 635–644.

[11] E. Alnazer, I. Georgievski, and M. Aiello, "On Bringing HTN Domains Closer to Reality-The Case of Satellite and Rover Domains", in *SPARK workshop in ICAPS*, 2022.

[12] I. Georgievski, "Conceptualising Software Development Lifecycle for Engineering AI Planning Systems", in *CAIN*, IEEE, 2023, pp. 88–89.

[13] E. Alnazer, I. Georgievski, and M. Aiello, "Risk Awareness in HTN Planning", *arXiv preprint arXiv:2204.10669*, 2022.

[14] D. Höller *et al.*, "HDDL: An Extension to PDDL for Expressing Hierarchical Planning Problems", in *AAAI conference on artificial intelligence*, AAAI Press, 2020, pp. 9883–9891.

[15] J. R. Silva, J. M. Silva, and T. S. Vaquero, "Formal Knowledge Engineering for Planning: Pre and Post-Design Analysis", *Knowledge Engineering Tools and Techniques for AI Planning*, pp. 47–65, 2020.

[16] I. Georgievski, "Hierarchical planning definition language", University of Groningen, Tech. Rep. JBI 2013-12-3, 2013.

[17] T. S. Vaquero, J. R. Silva, F. Tonidandel, and J. C. Beck, "itSIMPLE: Towards an Integrated Design System for Real Planning Applications", *KER*, vol. 28, no. 2, pp. 215–230, 2013.

[18] T. S. Vaquero, J. R. Silva, J. C. Beck, *et al.*, "Improving Planning Performance Through Post-Design Analysis", in *KEPS*, 2010, pp. 45–52.

[19] D. Pellier and H. Fiorino, "From Classical to Hierarchical: Benchmarks for the HTN Track of the International Planning Competition", *arXiv preprint arXiv:2103.05481*, 2021.

[20] F. D. S. Cividanes, M. G. V. Ferreira, and F. de Novaes Kucinskis, "An Extended HTN Language for Onboard Planning and Acting Applied to a Goal-Based Autonomous Satellite", *AESS*, vol. 36, no. 8, pp. 32–50, 2021.

[21] M. D. Rodríguez-Moreno, D. Borrajo, and D. Meziat, "An AI Planning-Based Tool for Scheduling Satellite Nominal Operations", *AI Magazine*, vol. 25, no. 4, pp. 9–9, 2004.

[22] F. Jimoh, L. Chrpa, T. L. McCluskey, and S. Shah, "Towards Application of Automated Planning in Urban Traffic Control", in *ITSC 2013*, IEEE, 2013, pp. 985–990.

[23] M. Vallati, D. Magazzeni, B. De Schutter, L. Chrpa, and T. McCluskey, "Efficient Macroscopic Urban Traffic Models for Reducing Congestion: A PDDL+ Planning Approach", in *AAAI conference on artificial intelligence*, AAAI Press, 2016, pp. 3188–3194.

[24] M. Gulić, R. Olivares, and D. Borrajo, "Using Automated Planning for Traffic Signals Control", *PROMET-Traffic&Transportation*, vol. 28, no. 4, pp. 383–391, 2016.

[25] T. McCluskey and M. Vallati, "Embedding Automated Planning within Urban Traffic Management Operations", in *ICAPS*, AAAI Press, 2017, pp. 391–399.

[26] F. Ivankovic, M. Roveri, *et al.*, "Planning with Global State Constraints for Urban Traffic Control", in *CEUR-WS.org*, CEUR-WS, 2021, pp. 1–5.

[27] T. X. Lin, M. Hou, C. R. Edwards, M. Cox, and F. Zhang, "Bounded Cost HTN Planning for Marine Autonomy", in *Global Oceans 2020: Singapore–US Gulf Coast*, IEEE, 2020, pp. 1–6.

[28] J. J. Kiam, P. Bercher, and A. Schulte, "Temporal Hierarchical Task Network Planning with Nested Multi-Vehicle Routing Problems — A Challenge to be Resolved", in *HPlan Workshop in ICAPS*, 2021, pp. 71–75.

[29] E. Turan, S. Speretta, and E. Gill, "Autonomous Navigation for deep Space Small Satellites: Scientific and Technological Advances", *Acta Astronautica*, vol. 193, pp. 56–74, 2022.

[30] D. Long and M. Fox, "The 3rd International Planning Competition: Results and Analysis", *JAIR*, vol. 20, pp. 1–59, 2003.

[31] C. Powell, C. S. Ruf, S. Gleason, and S. C. Rafkin, "Sampled Together: Assessing the Value of Simultaneous Collocated Measurements for Optimal Satellite Configurations", *BAMS*, vol. 105, no. 1, E285–E296, 2024.

[32] V. Maggioni, C. Massari, and C. Kidd, "Errors and Uncertainties Associated with Quasiglobal Satellite Precipitation Products", in *Precipitation science*, Elsevier, 2022, pp. 377–390.

[33] G. A. Landis, S. G. Bailey, and R. Tischler, "Causes of Power-Related Satellite Failures", in *WCPEC*, IEEE, 2006, pp. 1943–1945.

[34] P. S. Morgan, "Fault Protection Techniques in JPL Spacecraft", in *ISHEM*, 2005.

[35] H.-S. Choi *et al.*, "Analysis of GEO Spacecraft Anomalies: Space Weather Relationships", *Space weather*, vol. 9, no. 6, 2011.

[36] R. Horne *et al.*, "Space Weather Impacts on Satellites and Forecasting the Earth's Electron Radiation Belts with SPACECAST", *Space Weather*, vol. 11, no. 4, pp. 169–186, 2013.

[37] C. C. Liu, S. G. Hosking, and M. G. Lenné, "Predicting Driver Drowsiness Using Vehicle Measures: Recent Insights and Future Challenges", *Journal of safety research*, vol. 40, no. 4, pp. 239–245, 2009.

[38] N. R. Council *et al.*, *Completing the Forecast: Characterizing and Communicating uncertainty for Better Decisions Using Weather and Climate Forecasts*. National Academies Press, 2006.

[39] *Enhancing Weather Information with Probability Forecasts*, https://shorturl.at/pvG03, Accessed: 2022-03-18, 2022.

[40] J. Antoun, M. E. Kabir, R. F. Atallah, and C. Assi, "A Data Driven Performance Analysis Approach for Enhancing the QoS of Public Charging Stations", *T-ITS*, vol. 23, no. 8, pp. 11 116–11 125, 2021.

[41] *Google Maps directions for driving from Erlangen to Stuttgart*, https://shorturl.at/cosW7, Accessed: 2025-08-18, 2025.

[42] *Google Maps directions for driving from from Erlangen to Stuttgart*, https://shorturl.at/cKVWX, Accessed: 2025-08-18, 2025.

[43] P. Farradyne, "Traffic Incident Management Handbook", *Prepared for Federal Highway Administration, Office of Travel Management*, 2000.

[44] I. Georgievski and M. Aiello, "Phantomisation in State-Based HTN Planning", in *ASPAI*, 2019, pp. 39–44.

A Comparative Study on Automated Expiry Date Extraction from Official Documents Using OCR and Image Preprocessing

Alaeddin Türkmen, Barış Bayram, Ahmet Çay, Zehra Hafızoğlu Gökdağ
Data Science Team
Hepsijet
Istanbul, Turkey
e-mail: {alaeddin.turkmen | baris.bayram | ahmet.cay | zehra.gokdag}@hepsijet.com

***Abstract*—Extracting expiry dates from official documents is a critical task in numerous administrative and compliance workflows. Traditionally performed manually, this process is time-consuming, error-prone, and costly at scale. In this study, we present a comparative evaluation of multiple optical character recognition (OCR) engines combined with a diverse set of image preprocessing techniques to automate expiry date extraction from scanned and photographed documents, including insurance policies, identity cards, licenses, and inspection reports. A dataset of manually annotated portable document format (PDF) and joint photographic experts group (JPEG) files was used for benchmarking. Each image was processed using various transformations. Extracted texts were parsed using comprehensive regular expression patterns to identify date candidates, from which the latest valid date was selected as the predicted expiry. Our findings indicate that SuryaOCR, particularly when applied to unprocessed raw images, consistently outperformed other configurations, substantially reducing the need for manual intervention.**

Keywords-OCR; Automated Document Processing; Image Preprocessing.

I. INTRODUCTION

Extracting expiry dates from official documents is a fundamental task in numerous administrative, regulatory, and compliance workflows. Documents, such as driver's licenses, identity cards, insurance policies, and inspection certificates often contain expiry periods that must be accurately recorded and tracked. In many organizations, this information is still collected manually, a process that is time-consuming, error-prone, and difficult to scale.

Optical Character Recognition (OCR) technologies have emerged as a practical solution for automating the extraction of textual content from scanned or photographed documents. While OCR has proven effective in many domains, its performance can vary significantly depending on document structure, image quality, and the specific recognition model employed [1]. Furthermore, expiry dates are not always consistently formatted or positioned and may appear in multiple languages, be partially obscured by stamps, seals or other occlusions, making the extraction task particularly sensitive to errors in both recognition and post-processing.

To improve accuracy and robustness, OCR pipelines are often combined with image preprocessing techniques aimed at enhancing textual features. However, there is a common but largely untested assumption that preprocessing universally improves OCR performance. As in Björkman's study [2], especially in structured and high-quality documents, preprocessing may sometimes distort visual features rather than enhance them.

This study addresses these challenges by proposing a comparative framework for automated expiry date extraction, focusing on multilingual and partially occluded real-world administrative documents. The study was conducted to determine the expiry dates of the employment documents of couriers who started working at Hepsijet, a logistics company. We evaluate the performance of three OCR engines—SuryaOCR, EasyOCR, and Pytesseract—across ten different image preprocessing techniques. The experiments are conducted on a diverse dataset of real-world administrative documents, each manually annotated with ground-truth expiry dates. Extracted texts are parsed using carefully crafted, language-aware regular expression patterns, and the latest valid date is selected as the predicted output.

Our results show that SuryaOCR, particularly when applied to raw (unprocessed) images, significantly outperforms other configurations. In contrast, many preprocessing techniques negatively impact accuracy, challenging the assumption that preprocessing is always beneficial. This paper contributes an empirical evaluation of OCR-preprocessing combinations for expiry date extraction under multilingual and occlusion conditions, offers practical insights into building more reliable automated document processing pipelines for real-world deployments.

The remainder of this paper is organized as follows. Section 2 reviews related work on OCR-based date extraction and image preprocessing techniques. Section 3 describes the dataset, including multilingual and occluded document samples, as well as the preprocessing methods, OCR engines evaluated and evaluation procedure. Section 4 as Results and Discussion, presents performance comparison across OCR engines, impact of preprocessing, error analysis and limitations & observations. Section 5 concludes the study with key findings, practical recommendations for real-world deployment, and directions for future research.

II. RELATED WORK

OCR has long evolved from rule-based systems like Tesseract to deep-learning approaches tailored for complex, real-world scenarios. Kshetry et al. introduced a modified adaptive-thresholding method that uses the dominant pixel intensity within text regions to enhance contrast, showing measurable gains in PyTesseract accuracy on photographs [3]. El Harraj and Raissouni designed a nonparametric pipeline—combining local brightness normalization, grayscale conversion, unsharp masking, and global binarization—that significantly improved OCR performance on mobile-captured documents [4]. Dias and Lopes applied multi-objective parameter tuning of preprocessing filters (adaptive thresholding, bilateral filtering, morphological opening) on typewritten heritage documents, demonstrating that the effectiveness of preprocessing depends on document typology [5]. Kavin and Shirley focus on automating the extraction of batch numbers and expiration dates from pharmaceutical packaging using OCR. To improve recognition performance, the authors employ preprocessing techniques and validate extracted data through rule-based checks. Their system, tested on a diverse medical image dataset, demonstrates potential for reducing manual entry errors and enhancing patient safety in healthcare workflows [6].

More recently, Tavares systematically evaluated preprocessing techniques—grayscale conversion, contrast limited adaptive histogram equalization (CLAHE), and bilateral filtering—on license plate recognition pipelines and reported that combining CLAHE with bilateral filtering yielded the highest OCR accuracy under varied lighting [7]. Complementing this, a study in a controlled refrigerator-monitoring context tested multiple open-source OCR engines, integrating on-device preprocessing to improve robustness in suboptimal lighting, and found that tailored preprocessing was essential for capturing reliable expiry date text [8].

Beyond classical preprocessing, deep-learning approaches specifically addressing expiry date recognition are emerging. Florea and Rebedea developed a convolutional neural network (CNN) based model combined with synthetic data to improve recognition of expiry dates on food packaging, reporting a 9.4% accuracy boost over text-only baselines [9].

Emel, Terzioğlu, and Özkan address the variability in invoice structures by introducing a three-stage framework for date extraction comprising custom object detection, OCR, and regular expressions. Leveraging the YOLOv8 model for object detection and PaddleOCR for text recognition, the study presents a robust pipeline that adapts to diverse invoice formats. The authors emphasize the effectiveness of combining modern detection models with traditional parsing techniques to enhance accuracy in document processing [10].

Other research leverages scene-text detection networks (e.g., maximally stable extremal regions (MSER) detectors, TextBoxes++) to isolate date regions before OCR, often combined with deep sequence decoders like CRNN, yielding more robust extraction in cluttered environments [11]. While these studies explore individual OCR engines, preprocessing pipelines, or date detection networks, few perform a controlled comparison across multiple OCR engines *and* preprocessing methods within a unified framework—especially for structured expiry dates in administrative documents. Our work closes this gap by empirically evaluating combinations of SuryaOCR, EasyOCR, and PyTesseract with ten established preprocessing techniques on a real-world annotated dataset, thus providing practical insights for optimizing end-to-end expiry-date extraction workflows.

III. Methodology

This study proposes a comparative framework to identify the optimal combination of OCR engine and image preprocessing technique to extract the latest valid date from scanned document images. The aim is to simulate real-world conditions in administrative and regulatory domains, where expiry dates, such as expiration or renewal deadlines must be accurately identified from heterogeneous document formats.

A dataset of real documents with manually labeled ground-truth expiry dates is processed through multiple OCR pipelines, each involving a different preprocessing technique. The extracted textual content is parsed using carefully designed regular expression patterns to identify and retrieve date entities. The maximum (latest) date extracted from each OCR output is compared to the ground truth to assess accuracy. The evaluation results across combinations enable the selection of the most effective OCR + preprocessing strategy. The general flow is shown in Figure 1.

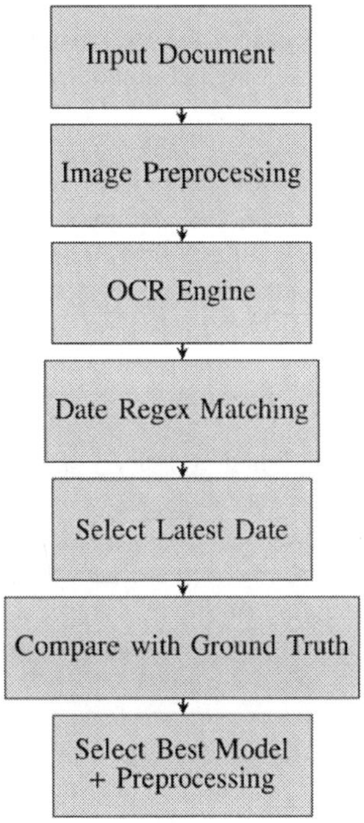

Figure 1. Overview of the processing pipeline: from input documents to model evaluation and selection.

A. Dataset Description

The dataset comprises 1,000 real-world documents in PDF and JPEG formats, sourced exclusively from a single logistics company's internal records. These documents include photos taken with varying lighting, contrast, noise, and distance, screenshots, rotated documents. The seven documents demonstrating the couriers' ability to perform their jobs when they first begin work:

- Vehicle insurance policies
- Driver's licenses (Shown in Fig. 2)
- Identity cards
- Health and liability insurance documents
- Psychotechnical evaluation reports
- Vehicle inspection certificates
- Commercial cargo operating certificate

Each document is manually annotated with its true expiry date (e.g., expiration or renewal date), allowing for quantitative evaluation of OCR-based extraction.

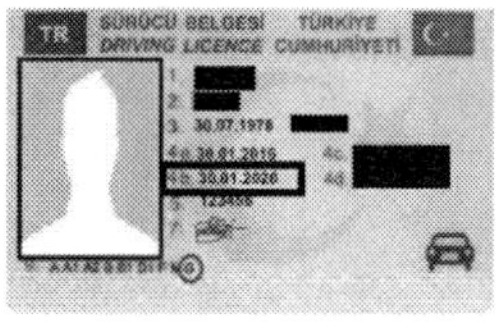

Figure 2. One of the sample employment documents

B. OCR Engines

Three open source and free OCR engines were selected to represent a diverse range of architectures and recognition methodologies:

1) SuryaOCR: SuryaOCR [12] is an open-source document layout analysis and OCR framework built on top of deep learning-based detection and recognition pipelines in more than 90 languages. It utilizes transformer-based models for layout-aware text detection and recognition. It consists of the EfficientViT [13] based detection model and the Donut [14] based recognition model. SuryaOCR is particularly well-suited for structured document processing tasks where field localization improves extraction accuracy.

2) EasyOCR: EasyOCR [15] is a deep learning-based OCR engine that supports over 80 languages and is widely used for both scene text and scanned document recognition. The model operates through three main stages: feature extraction, sequence labeling, and decoding. In the first stage, visual features are extracted from the input image using convolutional neural networks, such as Visual Geometry Group (VGG) and residual network (ResNet). These extracted features are then processed through Long Short-Term Memory (LSTM) networks, which are capable of modeling sequential dependencies and capturing contextual information across character sequences. Finally, the output is decoded using the Connectionist Temporal Classification (CTC) algorithm, which is well-suited for sequence-to-sequence tasks with unknown alignments between input and target sequences. The model architecture is implemented on top of the deep-text-recognition-benchmark framework, allowing for robust training across various datasets and enhancing EasyOCR's adaptability to diverse document types and layouts.

3) Pytesseract: Pytesseract is a Python wrapper for the Tesseract OCR engine [16], originally developed by HP and now maintained by Google. Tesseract operates using a classical OCR pipeline with optional LSTM support in newer versions. It supports a wide variety of configurations and preprocessing steps but is more sensitive to noise and skew compared to modern deep learning models.

Each OCR engine was tested independently with every image processing variant described in the following section.

C. Image Preprocessing Techniques

To investigate the influence of image quality and structure on OCR performance, a variety of preprocessing techniques were applied. These transformations aim to enhance features relevant for text recognition while reducing noise and artifacts. Each technique was implemented using either OpenCV or PIL (Pillow), depending on availability.

The preprocessing methods used are:

1) Raw: The original image is passed to the OCR engine without modification.

2) Grayscale: The image is converted to a single-channel grayscale format to remove color variations.

3) Binary Thresholding: Fixed thresholding is applied (default threshold = 150), converting pixels below the threshold to black and others to white. The value of 150 was selected based on preliminary experiments on a small validation subset, where it yielded the highest average OCR character accuracy compared to alternative values (100, 128, 180).

4) Adaptive Thresholding: A Gaussian-based adaptive threshold is used to binarize the image in varying lighting conditions.

5) Contrast Enhancement: Global contrast is increased using a scaling factor (default = 2.0). A factor of 2.0 consistently enhanced text visibility without introducing excessive noise or halo effects around characters, thereby improving OCR readability for most document types in the dataset.

6) Sharpening: Image sharpness is enhanced to accentuate text edges.

7) Noise Reduction: Gaussian blur is applied to reduce background noise.

8) Otsu Thresholding: An automatic threshold value is calculated based on Otsu's method for optimal binarization.

9) Morphological Operations: Operations, such as opening and dilation are applied to remove noise and enhance text connectivity.

10) Deskewing: The image is deskewed by calculating the rotation angle of the largest text contour and rotating accordingly.

Each technique was applied in isolation, yielding multiple versions of each document image. These versions were fed independently into the OCR engines, resulting in a combinatorial evaluation framework. If the date is not extracted after each recognition process, the image is rotated 90, 180 and 270 degrees in order to prevent the documents from being loaded at different angles and then fed back to the model.

D. Date Pattern Matching and Extraction

Following OCR-based text extraction, a rule-based pattern matching module was applied to identify all occurrences of dates within the recognized text. This is because the latest date recorded in the company documents represented the expiry date of the document. To ensure broad coverage across diverse document formats and languages, a comprehensive set of regular expression (regex) patterns was implemented. These patterns were designed to capture both numeric and textual date formats commonly found in official documents.

The date formats targeted include, but are not limited to:

- **Day/Month/Year (with slashes):**
  Examples: `01/01/2023`, `15/12/2021`
  Pattern: `\d{1,2}/\d{1,2}/\d{4}`
- **Day.Month.Year (with dots):**
  Examples: `01.01.2023`, `5.6.2020`
  Pattern: `\d{1,2}\.\d{1,2}\.\d{4}`
- **Year-Month-Day (ISO format):**
  Examples: `2023-06-19`, `2020-01-01`
  Pattern: `\d{4}-\d{2}-\d{2}`
- **Day-Month-Year (with dashes or commas):**
  Examples: `01-01-2023`, `15,12,2021`
  Pattern: `\d{1,2}[-,\.]\d{1,2}[-,\.]\d{4}`
- **Written month names (Turkish or English):**
  Examples: `15 Mart 2022`, `3 July 2021`
  Patterns:
  `\d{1,2} (Ocak|Şubat|...|Aralık) \d{4}`
  `\d{1,2} (January|...|December) \d{4}`

Additionally, expanded patterns were included to accommodate common inconsistencies:

- Omission of leading zeros (e.g., `1/1/2023` vs. `01/01/2023`)
- Use of mixed or nonstandard separators (e.g., `12.03/2023`, `15-02,2021`)
- Interchangeable date orderings (e.g., `YYYY/MM/DD` and `DD/MM/YYYY`)

In total, over 15 regular expression rules were crafted to support a wide variety of layout and formatting inconsistencies often observed in scanned or photographed documents.

After identifying all candidate date strings, each is parsed into a standardized date object. The latest (chronologically maximum) valid date is then selected as the document's predicted expiry date.

This prediction is subsequently compared to the manually annotated ground truth date to assess correctness for each combination of OCR engine and preprocessing method.

E. Evaluation Procedure

The evaluation of system performance was based on the accuracy of the predicted expiry date compared to a manually annotated ground truth. For each document processed through a specific combination of OCR engine and image preprocessing technique, the latest date identified via regular expression matching was interpreted as the predicted expiration date.

To quantify performance, this predicted date was directly compared to the annotated ground truth date. A prediction was considered correct only if the extracted date exactly matched the reference value, including day, month, and year components. No partial matches were accepted in order to maintain a strict and interpretable evaluation criterion. This is important to clearly determine the official expiry date of employment documents. Therefore, performance was measured with a strict accuracy metric focused on exact matching. This binary assessment (correct/incorrect) enabled the computation of accuracy for each OCR-preprocessing pair as the ratio of correctly predicted dates to the total number of documents evaluated.

To ensure robustness, the evaluation was conducted across all documents for each unique (OCR engine + preprocessing method) configuration. The resulting accuracy scores were then analyzed to identify performance patterns and rank the combinations according to their effectiveness in reliable date extraction. In addition to overall accuracy, qualitative observations regarding systematic failure cases—such as common misread characters, formatting inconsistencies, or model-specific artifacts—were documented to support deeper insights into the limitations and sensitivities of each approach.

IV. Results and Discussion

The evaluations and discussions about the results of the study are as follows.

A. Performance Comparison Across OCR Engines

The results demonstrate considerable variation in performance among the three evaluated OCR engines. The output of all model+preprocessing combinations is in Table 1. SuryaOCR yielded the highest overall accuracy, reaching 0.661 when applied to raw document images. EasyOCR followed with a maximum of 0.533, while Pytesseract remained below 0.37 across all configurations.

These differences can be attributed to the architectural choices and modeling paradigms employed by each engine. SuryaOCR is based on recent transformer vision architectures, such as EfficientViT and Donut, both of which are optimized for visually structured documents and capable of capturing long-range spatial dependencies. These models have been shown to perform well even when textual information is embedded in dense layouts or accompanied by background noise.

EasyOCR, in contrast, utilizes a convolutional neural network for visual feature extraction, followed by a recurrent LSTM layer for sequence modeling, and a CTC decoder for transcribing sequences. While this approach is well-suited to natural scene text and moderately structured inputs, it may be more sensitive to the kinds of layout variation and dense text regions observed in certain administrative documents.

Pytesseract, which serves as a Python wrapper for the classical Tesseract OCR engine, does not rely on deep learning-based visual reasoning. Instead, it applies rule-based heuristics and pattern matching for layout detection and character recognition. While effective in clearly scanned and uniformly formatted documents, its limitations become apparent under inconsistent lighting, noise, or structural distortion. Its comparatively low performance across all preprocessing techniques likely stems from this lack of adaptive learning mechanisms.

Overall, the superior performance of SuryaOCR suggests that modern vision transformers provide a robust foundation for text extraction tasks where document formatting is dense but consistent, as in the case of many official forms.

TABLE I
ACCURACY OF OCR MODELS WITH DIFFERENT PREPROCESSING TECHNIQUES

Model + Preprocessing	Accuracy
SuryaOCR	
Raw	**0.661**
Grayscale	0.644
Sharpening	0.619
Denoise	0.606
Contrast	0.558
Deskewing	0.528
Otsu	0.431
Morphological	0.424
Binary	0.424
Adaptive	0.253
EasyOCR	
Raw	0.533
Grayscale	0.518
Sharpening	0.510
Contrast	0.479
Deskewing	0.442
Otsu	0.343
Binary	0.343
Morphological	0.343
Denoise	0.377
Adaptive	0.132
Pytesseract	
Raw	0.365
Grayscale	0.348
Sharpening	0.328
Contrast	0.317
Deskewing	0.312
Denoise	0.307
Otsu	0.283
Binary	0.274
Morphological	0.274
Adaptive	0.066

B. Impact of Preprocessing

The influence of image preprocessing was found to be mixed and often detrimental. For all three OCR engines, raw images consistently resulted in better performance than their preprocessed counterparts. In SuryaOCR, grayscale and sharpening filters yielded only marginal drops in accuracy, while other operations, such as adaptive thresholding, morphological transformations, and deskewing led to substantial degradation in recognition quality.

This trend was even more pronounced in EasyOCR and Pytesseract, where most preprocessing techniques reduced accuracy significantly. Adaptive thresholding, for instance, decreased EasyOCR's performance to as low as 0.132, and even further in Pytesseract. These findings indicate that for structured and high-quality printed documents, preprocessing may distort textual features rather than enhance them, potentially disrupting the models' learned representations or rule-based heuristics.

It is likely that the preprocessing operations, particularly those designed for low-quality or noisy inputs, interfere with the sharp edges and uniform backgrounds typically found in scanned or photographed administrative forms. Therefore, the assumption that preprocessing universally improves OCR quality does not hold in this context, where the majority of documents are already visually clean and consistently formatted.

C. Error Analysis

A manual inspection of incorrect predictions revealed several common sources of error. In some cases, the OCR engine partially recognized the date field, extracting only the day and month, or misinterpreted the format due to spacing or font irregularities. In others, the algorithm erroneously selected unrelated date fields, such as print dates or issuance dates, rather than the intended expiry date. This issue was particularly evident in documents containing multiple date fields in similar visual prominence.

Additionally, the dataset consisted of 1000 randomly selected document images, which were acquired through a mix of scanning and mobile photography. Consequently, some samples exhibited poor visual quality due to factors, such as motion blur, shadow artifacts, low resolution, or uneven lighting. In several instances, the actual expiry date was illegible to both the OCR engine and human annotators, especially in heavily degraded or partially occluded regions of the document. These visual defects likely contributed to both false positives and false negatives.

Another noteworthy factor is the diversity of document types included in the dataset, such as identity cards, driver's licenses, insurance forms, and inspection reports. Each category possesses distinct structural patterns, font styles, and positional layouts of the expiry date. This heterogeneity may have introduced further complexity to the task, particularly for OCR engines that lack document-type-specific tuning. For example, dates on vehicle inspection reports are typically handwritten or stamped, whereas those on ID cards are printed in machine-readable zones, requiring different recognition strategies.

Together, these sources of error highlight the need for document-aware post-processing techniques, including context-driven date selection, region-of-interest filtering, or the integration of layout prediction models to disambiguate visually similar fields.

D. Limitations and Observations

The evaluation was conducted on a diverse and realistic corpus of administrative documents. However, several limitations must be acknowledged. Firstly, the ground truth for each document included only a single expiry date, whereas documents often contain multiple dates, any of which could be visually or semantically plausible. This binary evaluation framework may have underestimated the practical utility of certain OCR outputs that extracted valid but unintended date fields.

Secondly, while various preprocessing techniques were systematically tested, the choice of parameters, such as kernel sizes or contrast factors, was kept fixed across documents. A more adaptive preprocessing pipeline might yield improved results, particularly if guided by document layout classification or confidence estimation.

Finally, the evaluation focused solely on matching extracted date strings with ground truth labels, without incorporating additional semantic validation or natural language context. Future extensions could explore hybrid models that combine

OCR with named entity recognition or multimodal transformers trained to reason over both visual and textual cues.

These limitations notwithstanding, the results provide useful insights into the practical performance boundaries of common OCR frameworks and preprocessing strategies when applied to real-world administrative records.

V. Conclusion and Future Work

This study investigated the effectiveness of various OCR engines and image preprocessing techniques in extracting the expiry date from structured administrative documents, such as insurance certificates, identification cards, vehicle inspection reports, and similar official records. The proposed system demonstrated a significant automation potential, achieving up to 66.1

Among the evaluated models, transformer-based SuryaOCR exhibited superior performance, particularly when used on raw document images. Contrary to common expectations, most preprocessing operations, such as thresholding, noise reduction, and morphological filtering led to diminished accuracy. These findings suggest that for visually clean and structured documents, aggressive preprocessing may disrupt rather than enhance text recognizability. This insight can inform future system designs by reducing unnecessary computational overhead related to image enhancement stages.

Despite promising results, several avenues for improvement remain. First, model accuracy may be further increased through task-specific fine-tuning of OCR engines using domain-relevant training data. Especially in cases where expiry dates follow predictable patterns in fixed regions of the document, integrating visual layout modeling or region-based text filtering could improve both precision and recall. Moreover, hybrid approaches that combine rule-based post-processing with semantic filtering (e.g., recognizing keywords, such as "Valid Until") may aid in disambiguating among multiple date fields.

Handling exceptional cases also remains a critical consideration. In particular, documents that are uploaded incorrectly—either by being outside the supported set of document types or by omitting the required expiry date field—can lead to failed or misleading outputs. To address this, a document classification step could be introduced prior to OCR processing to ensure compatibility. Furthermore, if no valid date is detected, the system can be configured to trigger a fallback workflow, such as alerting human reviewers or requesting resubmission. Confidence scoring and anomaly detection methods may also be leveraged to flag uncertain predictions, reducing the risk of silent failure in high-stakes applications.

Due to the scope of this study, the types of documents used were limited, and the validity dates could be identified using regular expression patterns. In future work, we plan to expand the dataset to include a broader range of document types and languages, and to evaluate the inclusion of layout-aware deep learning models. Furthermore, we aim to enhance the system's intelligence by enabling it to recognize the specific type of each document. Additionally, integrating Large Language Models (LLMs) or vision transformer models for semantic validation and context-based extraction of date fields represents a promising direction for improving robustness in real-world deployments.

References

[1] A. Alaei, V. Bui, D. Doermann, and U. Pal, "Document image quality assessment: A survey", *ACM computing surveys*, vol. 56, no. 2, pp. 1–36, 2023.

[2] J. Björkman, *Evaluation of the effects of different preprocessing methods on ocr results from images with varying quality*, 2019.

[3] R. L. Kshetry, "Image preprocessing and modified adaptive thresholding for improving ocr", *arXiv preprint arXiv:2111.14075*, 2021.

[4] A. El Harraj and N. Raissouni, "Ocr accuracy improvement on document images through a novel pre-processing approach", *arXiv preprint arXiv:1509.03456*, 2015.

[5] M. Dias and C. T. Lopes, "Optimization of image processing algorithms for character recognition in cultural typewritten documents", *arXiv preprint arXiv:2311.15740*, 2023.

[6] S. Kavin and C. Shirley, "Ocr-based extraction of expiry dates and batch numbers in medicine packaging for error-free data entry", in *2024 7th International Conference on Circuit Power and Computing Technologies (ICCPCT)*, IEEE, vol. 1, 2024, pp. 278–283.

[7] R. A. Tavares, "Comparison of image preprocessing techniques for vehicle license plate recognition using ocr: Performance and accuracy evaluation", *arXiv preprint arXiv:2410.13622*, 2024.

[8] K. Hosozawa, R. H. Wijaya, T. D. Linh, H. Seya, M. Arai, T. Maekawa, and K. Mizutani, "Recognition of expiration dates written on food packages with open source ocr", *International Journal of Computer Theory and Engineering*, vol. 10, no. 5, pp. 170–174, 2018.

[9] V. Florea and T. Rebedea, "Expiry date recognition using deep neural networks", *International Journal of User-System Interaction*, vol. 13, no. 1, pp. 1–17, 2020.

[10] M. H. Emel, M. Terzioğlu, and R. Özkan, "Efficient and accurate date extraction from invoices: A comprehensive three-step methodology integrating custom object detection, ocr, and refined regular expressions", *Advances in Artificial Intelligence Research*, vol. 4, no. 1, pp. 10–17, 2024.

[11] L. Gong, M. Yu, W. Duan, X. Ye, K. Gudmundsson, and M. Swainson, "A novel camera based approach for automatic expiry date detection and recognition on food packages", in *IFIP international conference on artificial intelligence applications and innovations*, Springer, 2018, pp. 133–142.

[12] V. Paruchuri and D. Team, "Surya: A lightweight document ocr and analysis toolkit", GitHub repository, 2025, [Online]. Available: https://github.com/VikParuchuri/surya (visited on 08/18/2025).

[13] H. Cai, J. Li, M. Hu, C. Gan, and S. Han, "Efficientvit: Multi-scale linear attention for high-resolution dense prediction", *arXiv preprint arXiv:2205.14756*, 2022.

[14] G. Kim, T. Hong, M. Yim, J. Nam, J. Park, J. Yim, W. Hwang, S. Yun, D. Han, and S. Park, "Ocr-free document understanding transformer", in *European Conference on Computer Vision*, Springer, 2022, pp. 498–517.

[15] JaidedAI, "Easyocr", GitHub repository, 2021, [Online]. Available: https://github.com/JaidedAI/EasyOCR (visited on 08/18/2025).

[16] R. Smith, "An overview of the tesseract ocr engine", in *ICDAR '07: Proceedings of the Ninth International Conference on Document Analysis and Recognition*, Washington, DC, USA: IEEE Computer Society, 2007, pp. 629–633, ISBN: 0-7695-2822-8.

Fuzzy Agent-Based Modelling and Simulation of Autonomous Vehicle Fleets for Automatic Baggage Handling in 4.0 Airports

Alain-Jérôme Fougères
ECAM Louis de Broglie
IT and Telecommunications Laboratory
Rennes, France
email: alain-jerome.fougeres@ecam-ldb.fr

Ouzna Oukacha
ECAM Louis de Broglie
IT and Telecommunications Laboratory
Rennes, France
email: ouzna.oukacha@ecam-ldb.fr

Moïse Djoko-Kouam
ECAM Louis de Broglie
IETR, UMR CNRS 6164
Rennes, France
email: moise.djoko-kouam@ecam-ldb.fr

Egon Ostrosi
UTBM
ERCOS/ELLIAD EA4661
Belfort 90010, France
email: egon.ostrosi@utbm.fr

Abstract— **Industry 4.0 offers a set of methods, techniques, tools, and technologies that are naturally relevant for the development of services in the airports of the future. Integrating these different concepts into an airport is not without its challenges, given the complexity of the systems in place. Modelling and simulation phases have therefore become essential to ensure the success of these integrations. In this paper, we presented a case study involving the simulation of autonomous vehicle fleets for baggage handling in a simplified airport, in which each vehicle is simulated by a fuzzy agent. We established a Unified Modeling Language (UML) model of the system, providing both static and dynamic views of the circuit and the vehicles. Three different strategies were tested, with the goal of determining the number of Autonomous Industrial Vehicles (AIV) that should circulate to handle the baggage arriving at the two entry points. Then, we presented our simulation results. These results allowed us to highlight the impact of various parameters, such as the number of simulations, the number of bags processed, the total simulation duration, and the total number of bags processed per hour.**

Keywords- automatic baggage handling; autonomous industrial vehicles; fuzzy agent-based simulation; airport 4.0.

I. INTRODUCTION

Industry 4.0 is the fourth industrial revolution after the invention of the steam engine, mechanization and mass production, computerization and robotization. It brings the concepts of the Internet of Things (IoT), Cyber-Physical Systems (CPS), Machine to Machine (M2M), and intelligent robotics, such as Autonomous Mobile Robots (AMR) or Autonomous Industrial Vehicles (AIV) [1]. Industry 4.0 assumes decentralized decision-making, interoperability, cyber assistance, predictive maintenance, eco-design and is user centred [2]. Industry 5.0 has complemented the previous one by amplifying the consideration of humans with Human machine connectivity and co-existence [3][4].

The deployment of fleets of autonomous vehicles (AMRs or AIVs) in the context of Airport 4.0 raises several challenges, all related to the actual level of autonomy of these "intelligent" vehicles: decision-making to maintain a required level of performance in carrying out tasks, traffic flow, vehicle localization, fault detection, collision avoidance, vehicle perception in changing environments, as well as acceptance by users and operators. Simulation, prior to the deployment of autonomous vehicles, makes it possible to consider the various constraints and requirements formulated by manufacturers and future airport users [5].

The main advantages of simulating the operations carried out by a fleet of autonomous industrial vehicles are the reduction of fleet development time and cost, the minimization of potential operational risks associated with the deployment of vehicles in a space shared with humans, but also the verification of fleet performance. This makes it possible to assess the feasibility of different scenarios for the circulation of autonomous vehicles at a strategic or operational level, the possibility of a rapid understanding of the operations carried out by these vehicles, the identification of improvements in the layout configurations of vehicle circulation areas [6], and safety assessment during coexistence and possible interactions between autonomous vehicles and human operators [7].

An autonomous baggage handling system is a complex and highly adaptive transportation system. So, different types of simulation frameworks and environments have been proposed for simulating complex systems involving autonomous vehicles (AMRs or AIVs), such as discrete event systems [8] or agent-based systems [9].

Many agent-based approaches are proposed for the modelling and simulation of autonomous vehicles [10]. They offer simulation contexts ranging from trajectory planning to optimal task allocation, while enabling collision and obstacle avoidance [11], addressing issues of traffic congestion, parking requirements, environmental implications or even the performance of autonomous vehicle systems [12].

One of the main problems of complex systems, such as automatic baggage handling systems in airports, results from the acquired or transmitted data, which may be uncertain, insufficient or available in a fragmented manner due to the dynamics of the environments and the variation of acquisition times. Fuzzy logic then appears as a good solution to model and simulate the uncertainty and the unknown in these complex and adaptive systems [13][14].

In [15][16], Zadeh defines fuzzy logic and the notion of fuzzy sets, introducing the notion of linguistic variables whose values are generally vague, fuzzy, or relative, such as "low", "medium", "high", "most", or "a certain number". By defining these linguistic variables (fuzzy sets), as well as rules using them (fuzzy rules), it is then possible to build Fuzzy Inference Systems (FIS).

Fuzzy set theory is therefore particularly suited to the processing of uncertain or imprecise information that should lead to decision-making by autonomous agents [17]. Also, the definition of fuzzy agents to manage the levels of imprecision and uncertainty involved in modelling the behaviour of simulated vehicles seems quite appropriate [18].

Fuzzy agents can track the evolution of fuzzy information from their environment and from the agents themselves. By interpreting this fuzzy information, they can act and interact within a fuzzy multi-agent system. Thus, a fuzzy agent can discriminate a fuzzy interaction value to assess its degree of affinity (or interest) with another fuzzy agent.

Moreover, most of the control tasks performed by autonomous mobile robots (simulated by agents or real) have been the subject of performance improvement studies using fuzzy logic: motion planning, navigation and obstacle avoidance [19]; path planning [20], localization [21], and intelligent management of energy consumption [22].

We believe it is useful to provide here some details about the research context that led to this publication. The academic collaboration between the authors, focusing on the dual theme of fuzzy logic and autonomous industrial vehicles, played an important role in the development of this article by combining expertise from each respective field. In addition, the industrial collaboration within the framework of the multi-partner collaborative project named ALPHA also had a significant place in this same research context. Thus, we find it important to share the following information regarding this second aspect: 1) the ALPHA project brought together a four-party consortium, including two industrial partners and two research laboratories; 2) the aim of the project was to identify and validate a mobile robotics solution for the transportation of unit baggage in airports; and 3) the ALPHA project focused particularly on two key challenges: on the one hand, optimizing an AGV fleet based on minimal energy consumption; on the other hand, minimizing the complexity of the robotic solution under the constraint of a large number of AGVs.

In this article, we start by presenting the context of fuzzy agent-based modelling and simulation. In Section 3, we propose a case study on simulation of autonomous vehicle fleets for baggage handling in a sample airport. Three strategies are presented with three different data sets. In Section 4, we analyse the results obtained by each of the strategies according to the performance criteria defined in the previous Section. Finally, we conclude on the proposed fuzzy agent-based modelling and simulation, and then we present the perspectives for improvement in the short term.

II. FUZZY AGENT-BASED MODELLING AND SIMULATION

We indicated in the introductory section that many agent-based approaches are proposed for the modelling and simulation of complex systems, such as autonomous vehicles. We further assume that, equipped with reasoning and decision-making capabilities based on fuzzy knowledge, agents could simulate more complex, but also more realistic, situations.

A. Fuzzy agent-based application modelling

The modelling of an agent-based system or application, often discussed from a process or methodological point of view [23], requires adopting a local vision, to respect the fact that each agent is responsible for their knowledge and actions (agent autonomy), which are often decentralized.

Different models can be used to propose a methodology for designing an agent-based application, including: an agent model, to define the characteristics of an agent; a task model, to represent the tasks that can be performed by agents; an expertise model, to describe the knowledge of agents; a coordination model, to define the protocols and interactions between agents; an organization model, to describe the organization of the agent society; or a communication model, to describe the interactions between agents and users. Our agent modelling work mainly refers to the Agent Unified Modeling Language (AUML) [24].

In [25], we proposed a four-phase agent-based system modelling method (Figure 1): (1) create use case diagrams (the services provided by the system); (2) for each use case, create sequence diagrams specifying the interactions (message exchanges and scheduling) between the agents involved in these reference cases; (3) from the sequence diagrams, which allowed us to identify the agents, the system objects and their interactions, create the class diagram: the objects are associated with classes, the messages exchanged (service requests between objects) are translated by operations on the classes, the parameters associated with the operations are translated into class attributes – this diagram can possibly be completed by a collaboration diagram; (4) from the class diagram, define the behaviour of each agent (agent class) by means of a state or activity diagram (we also used Petri nets). The description of the roles played by the different cooperative agents mainly focuses on collaboration and sequence diagrams. We subsequently integrated an expertise model into the previous method, particularly in the form of knowledge and fuzzy inference rules [26].

We are now testing the integration of learning capabilities into fuzzy agents in the form of a basic but generic neural network or reinforcement learning processes. This is to give agents the ability to better adapt in unforeseen situations during their modelling, and to adjust their fuzzy knowledge when extracting it from human experts is difficult or problematic (uncertain knowledge or approximate fuzzy modelling).

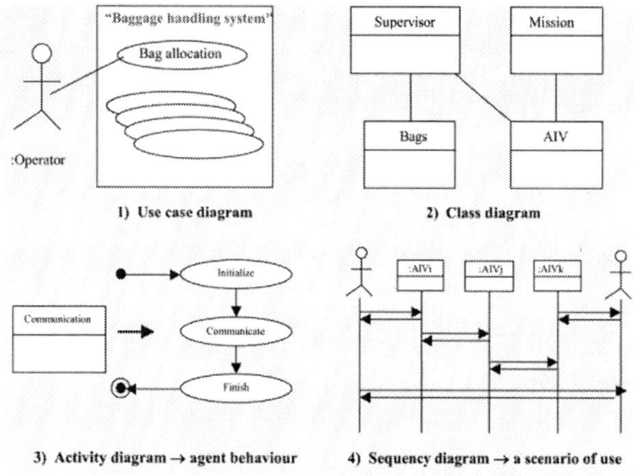

Figure 1. Agent-based system design: methodology adapted from AUML

B. *Fuzzy agent modelling*

An agent-based system is fuzzy if some of the agents that compose it have fuzzy behaviours or if the knowledge they use is fuzzy. This means that agents are modelled in such a way as to [18]:

- use fuzzy knowledge in their inferences; this knowledge consists of fuzzy linguistic variables, fuzzy linguistic values, and fuzzy rules [17];
- adopt fuzzy behaviours, following fuzzy inferences [27];
- and potentially implement fuzzy interactions, act in fuzzy organizations, or play fuzzy roles [28].

Formally, a fuzzy agent-based system (1) and the fuzzy agents that compose it (2) can be defined as follows:

$$\widetilde{M}_\alpha = <\widetilde{A},\widetilde{I},\widetilde{P},\widetilde{O}> \quad (1)$$

Where $\widetilde{A}$ is a set of fuzzy agents; $\widetilde{I}$ is a set of fuzzy interactions between fuzzy agents; $\widetilde{P}$ is a set of fuzzy roles that fuzzy agents can perform; $\widetilde{O}$ is a set of fuzzy organizations defined for fuzzy agents (subsets of strongly linked fuzzy agents).

$$\widetilde{\alpha}_i = \left\langle \Phi_{\Pi(\widetilde{\alpha}_i)}, \Phi_{\Delta(\widetilde{\alpha}_i)}, \Phi_{\Gamma(\widetilde{\alpha}_i)}, K_{\widetilde{\alpha}_i} \right\rangle \quad (2)$$

Where, for a fuzzy agent $\widetilde{\alpha}_i$, $\Phi_{\Pi(\widetilde{\alpha}_i)}$ is its function of observation; $\Phi_{\Delta(\widetilde{\alpha}_i)}$ is its function of decision; $\Phi_{\Gamma(\widetilde{\alpha}_i)}$ is its function of action; and $K_{\widetilde{\alpha}_i}$ is its set of fuzzy knowledge.

In the following case study, we will mainly develop fuzzy knowledge modelling. For the interested reader, we have extensively developed fuzzy modelling of other dimensions in the following articles [26][27][28][29].

III. Case study: Simulation of autonomous vehicle fleets for baggage handling

In this section, we present a case study of a baggage handling system in an airport using a fleet of autonomous vehicles. We will successively propose the agent model of vehicle behaviour, the fuzzy logic modelling of their decision rules, and three baggage handling strategies to discuss the performance obtained in the following section.

A. *Presentation of the case study*

The case study presented in this paper proposes the simulation of baggage handling in a basic airport with two baggage entry flows and two baggage exit flows. The mobile robots (AIV) in charge of baggage handling travel a loop circuit shown in Figure 2.a. The AIVs are simulated by fuzzy agents, and the airport circuit is represented by a directed graph. This graph has 17 nodes (Figure 2.b): node *P0* represents the parking lot, nodes *R1* and *R2* represent the 2 baggage pick-up points, nodes *D1* and *D2* represent the 2 baggage drop-off points, and the other 12 nodes *Pi* represent characteristic points of the circuit (curve start points, curve end points, convergence points and divergence points).

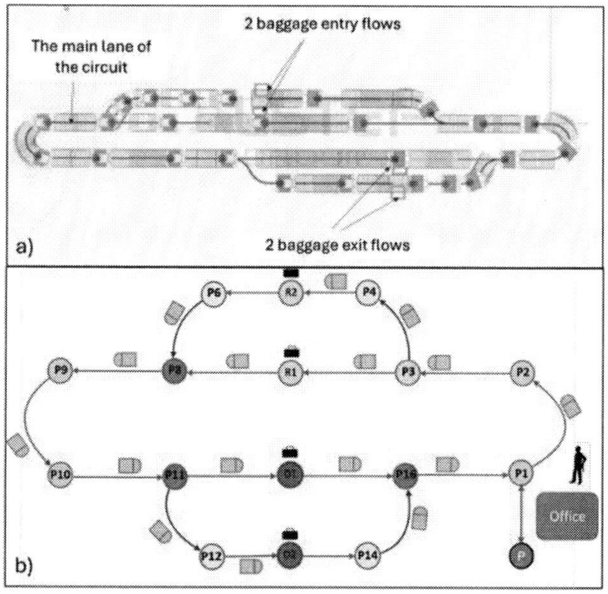

Figure 2. Simulation Application: a) the circuit, and b) the graph model

The application itself is developed in Python. Figure 3 presents its object and agent architecture in the form of a UML class diagram: static objects are represented in blue, and agents, therefore dynamic, are represented in red (only AIV agents are fuzzy agents). An infrastructure can be deployed in this environment. It includes a traffic plan and potentially active elements, such as beacons, tags, charging stations, etc. Static or dynamic obstacles (e.g., operators or broken-down AIVs) can also be activated in this simulation environment.

To study the performance of the solutions considered in this simulation, we defined the optimization system presented below (3): the objectives are to Minimize x, Maximize y, and Minimize z, where x is the number of AIVs, y is the baggage throughput per hour, and z is the recharge time of an AIV per hour (in ideal conditions where an AIV picks up one baggage each turn, a level of performance that we will analyse in the case study presented in Section 3, based on strategies deployed by the AIVs).

$$\begin{cases} 0 \leq x \leq Max(x) = {}^{L_{avg}}/_{d} \\ 0 \leq y \leq T_{avg} * Max(x) \\ 0 \leq z \leq 3600 \\ z = \left({}^{v_{avg}*3600}/_{C_{bat}}\right) * (t_0 + t_1) \\ T_0 = \left({}^{L_{avg}}/_{v_{avg}}\right) + (t_2 + t_3) \\ T_{avg} = {}^{(3600-z)}/_{T_0} \\ y = T_{avg} * x \end{cases} \quad (3)$$

Where $Max(x)$ is the maximum number of AIVs; L_{avg} is the average length of the circuit; d is the safety distance between 2 AIVs; C_{bat} is the average capacity of a battery; t_0 is the average charging time of a battery; t_1 is the average waiting time for a battery recharge; T_0 average duration of a circuit lap; t_2 is the time to pick up a bag; t_3 is the time to drop off a bag; T_{avg} is the average number of revolutions made by an AIV during one hour; and v_{avg} is the average speed of the AIVs on the circuit.

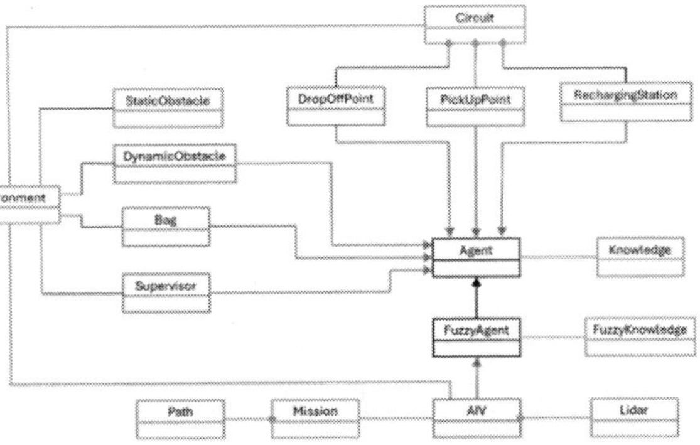

Figure 3. UML class-diagram of the fuzzy-agent based simulator.

An initial study focused on the sizing of the problem (traffic plan, number of AIVs, determination of applicable speeds, distances between AIVs, energy consumption of these AIVs, etc.) [5], followed by a Petri nets-based simulation of the AIV behaviour in function of strategies of baggage handling developed (Figure 4), allowed us to set the following parameters: $Max(x)=40$, $L_{avg}=313$, $v_{avg}=5$, $d=8$, $t_2=t_3=2$, and $z \approx 10\%$ of the AIVs operating time if t_1 is zero.

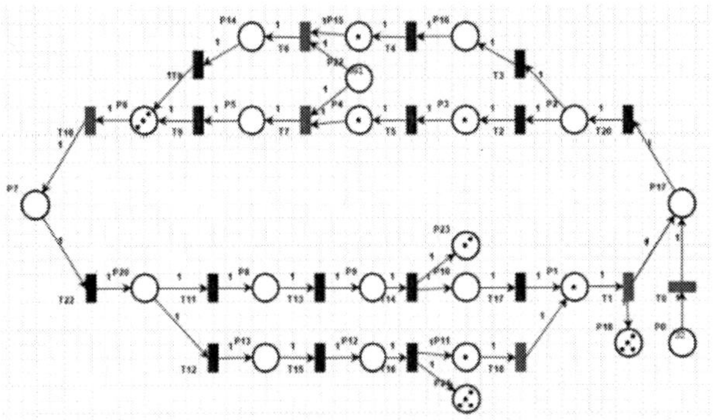

Figure 4. Petri net model of the circuit in Figure 2.a. It allows us to simulate a solution, while verifying that it retains the properties of liveness (non-blocking) and bounding of quantitative parameters such as the number of AGVs. The transitions in red indicate the possible evolution of the Petri net.

B. *AIV behaviour and their fuzzy knowledge*

As defined in the agent-based systems design methodology, one of the steps is to model the behaviour of the agents in the form of an activity or state diagram. The AIV agents in the simulation will have a behaviour adapted to the strategy implemented to process the baggage. Thus, Figure 5 presents the activity diagram of an AIV agent when it circulates according to the Round robin strategy (continuous looping if there is baggage to process).

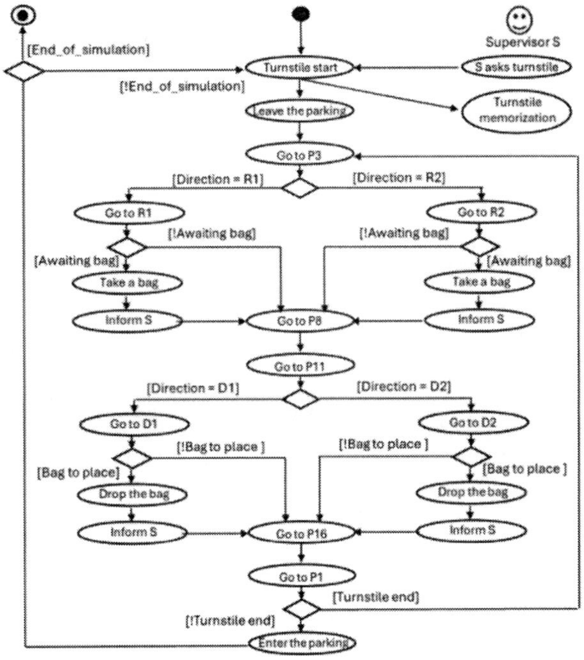

Figure 5. AIV behaviour based on "Round robin" strategy

AIVs are fuzzy agents that therefore have fuzzy knowledge. In this simulation, 2 types of fuzzy inferences are considered: the prediction of the number of AIVs that must circulate to process baggage, and the determination of the branch to choose to take a baggage (passage through R1 or R2).

For prediction, AIV agents have 3 linguistic variables (*NbBag, NbAIV, Prediction*, as shown in Figure 6) and 9 rules, such as (4):

IF *NbBag* ***IS*** *low* ***AND*** *NbAIV* ***IS*** *high*
THEN *Prediction* ***IS*** *highDecrease* (4)

As for the choice of branch *R1* or branch *R2*, the AIVs have 5 linguistic variables (*NbBagInR1, NbBagInR2, NbAIVToR1, NbAIVToR2, GoTo*, as shown in Figure 7) and 18 rules, such as (5):

IF *NbBagInR1* ***IS*** *low* ***AND*** *NbAIVToR1* ***IS*** *high*
THEN *GoTo* ***IS*** *R2* (5)

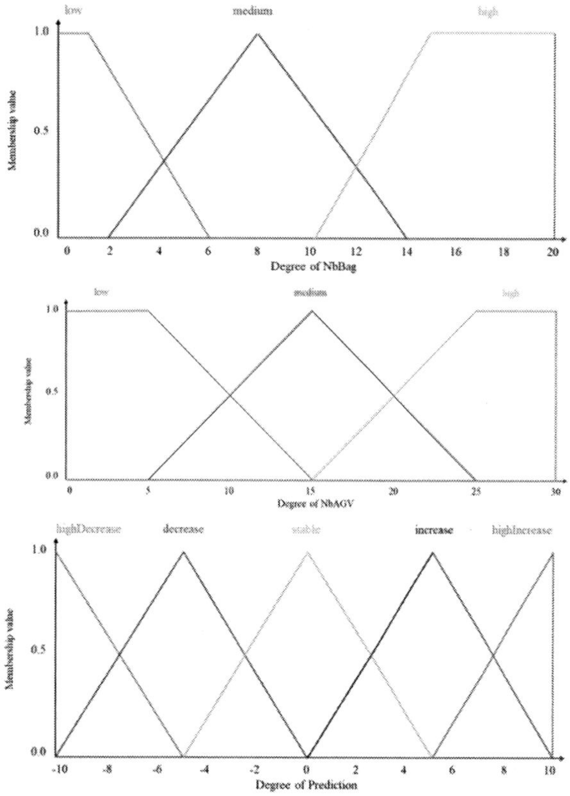

Figure 6. Linguistic variables to predict whether an AIV should circulate.

C. *The three considered strategies*

The goal here is to determine the number of AIVs that must circulate to process baggage arriving at both entry points. Three distinct strategies were simulated to test them and establish their performance on the system:

- **Round robin**. AIVs rotate around the circuit and pick up a bag if one is available on R1 or R2, depending on their route.
- **On-demand**. AIVs are assigned when baggage arrives and is available in the parking lot.
- **Fuzzy logic-based demand prediction**. The number of AIVs rotating around the circuit is calculated periodically based on predicted needs using fuzzy rules established by the operator. Other types of predictive strategies could be used, but as we have already shown the interest of fuzzy logic to efficiently solve this type of problem [30], we decided to develop this approach in this comparison of strategies.

Baggage arrival is a determining factor in the observable results for the three previous strategies. We have therefore defined different types of scenarios to cover many cases. Below we present the three main scenarios (without their variants):

- **Sc1 – Real data.** Baggage arrival is simulated based on aircraft arrivals at a sample airport, to better account for the variability of incoming baggage flow (high demand periods and low demand periods). These data cover a full day's traffic at the sample airport.

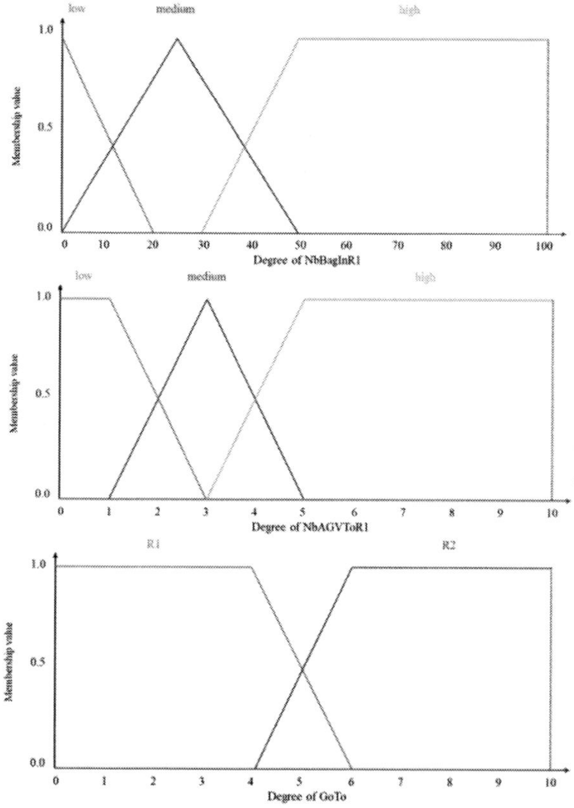

Figure 7. Linguistic variables for an AIV to choose one of the 2 branches.

- **Sc2 – Random Data**. Baggage arrival is randomly simulated over a period of one hour. Random data generation is performed upstream to create a single data set. This data set is then used to test the three strategies.

- **Sc3 – Mass data**. 1000 bags arrive continuously at the 2 entrances of the circuit. This involves performing a stress test for each strategy, regardless of the quality of each strategy's performance (e.g., a baggage waiting time threshold).

IV. RESULTS

Now, we present the results of the 9 simulations carried out according to the specifications formulated in the previous Section (3 scenarios x 3 strategies). The five performance criteria retained, with regard to the optimization system presented in (3), are: the duration of the simulation (i.e., the duration of processing of all baggage entering the simulated scenario), the number of baggage processed, the number of baggage processed per hour (throughput per hour), the number of circuit turns made by the AIVs to process all baggage, the average waiting time for baggage before being taken by an AIV, and the performance impact of AIV recharge times is estimated at 10% of AIV circulation time.

We will detail the results for each of the 6 criteria, then we will present the synthesis of these simulations.

Results regarding total simulation duration (Table 1). With the exception of the 1h scenario in random baggage flow, the Round robin strategy always has the longest duration, the On-demand and FL Prediction strategies are more variable, with a shorter duration for On-demand when the baggage flow is continuous (test Mass data), and a lower duration for FL Prediction when the flow is more variable (flow depending on the arrival of aircraft at test Real data). Both FL Prediction and On-demand strategies optimize the processing time by activating AIVs when baggage arrives by determining the right traffic branches, which is not the case for AIVs in the Round robin strategy.

Results regarding the total number of bags processed (Table 2). Two of the scenarios have a fixed number of bags (the test airport called Real data with a fixed number of bags of 1306, and the Mass data scenario with 1000 continuous bags); for the third scenario, with a random flow over 1 hour, the On-demand strategy is the least efficient (1864 bags), then the LF Prediction strategy (1956 bags), finally the most efficient is the Round robin strategy (2015 bags). On this criterion, the Round robin strategy is overall the most satisfactory, it is also on this criterion that it has its main advantage.

Results regarding the overall throughput of the 3 strategies (Table 3). The two strategies of Round robin and On-Demand have the worst overall results. In continuous and variable flows, the Round robin strategy performs poorly (respectively 1578 and 1713 bags/h). On the other hand, in random flow over 1 hour, the On-demand strategy performs the least (1864 bags/h). The average and overall flow rate is unquestionably the best with the Prediction strategy (1807 bags/h on average over the 3 scenarios).

Results regarding the total number of turns made by the AIVs (Table 4). For this criterion, the Round robin strategy is systematically the least efficient, and this significantly. 1664 rounds on average over the 3 scenarios for the Round robin strategy, against 1526 rounds on average for the FL Prediction strategy and 1390 rounds on average for the On-demand strategy. The average and overall number of AIV rounds is undoubtedly the best with the On-demand strategy (1390 rounds on average over the 3 scenarios); the allocation of an arriving bag to an AIV is indeed very efficient. For the FL Prediction strategy, the average results remain satisfactory (1526 rounds on average over the 3 scenarios), while those of the Round robin strategy are rather mediocre (1664 rounds on average over the 3 scenarios).

Results regarding the average waiting time for bags before being processed by an AIV (Table 5). For this criterion, the Round robin strategy is twice the least efficient (for the one-hour random flow and for the variable flow of the Real data test), and the On-demand strategy is the least efficient for the continuous flow of 1000 bags. The On-demand strategy gives very satisfactory results on average for the 3 scenarios (22 s average wait for a bag), and the FL Prediction strategy also gives satisfactory performances for the three scenarios (23 s average wait for a bag).

Results regarding the performance impact of AIV recharge times (Table 6). The AIVs run the same algorithm to determine whether they should recharge at a charging station located in the parking lot. The principles of the algorithm are as follows: 4 stations (corresponding to 10% of the 40 AIVs), recharge every 10 laps of the circuit (every 10 x 66s = 660s, on average), recharge if possible, when the AIVs are in the parking lot and recharge all the AIVs at the end of the simulation. Table 6 gives the results for a simulation with scenario 2 (one-hour simulation in random mode): number of recharges, total recharge time, and total duration of the simulation (3600s + final recharge for the AIVs to be fully charged again). The results provided by the on-demand strategy are the best, although at the cost of many recharges (when the AIVs return to the parking lot). The FL Prediction strategy offers a good compromise with interesting results that can be further improved by adjusting the values of the linguistic variables used in the fuzzy rules.

TABLE I. SIMULATION DURATION FOR THE 3 STRATEGIES (S)

Scenarios	Real data	Random data	Mass data
Round robin	2744	3600	2280
On-demand	2686	3600	2196
FL prediction	2515	3600	2252

TABLE II. NUMBER OF BAGS PROCESSED BY THE 3 STRATEGIES

Scenarios	Real data	Random data	Mass data
Round robin	1306	2015	1000
On-demand	1306	1864	1000
FL prediction	1306	1956	1000

TABLE III. FLOW RATE OF THE THREE STRATEGIES (bags/h)

Scenarios	Real data	Random data	Mass data
Round robin	1713	2015	1578
On-demand	1750	1864	1639
FL prediction	1868	1956	1597

TABLE IV. NUMBER OF TURNS COMPLETED BY THE AIVS

Scenarios	Real data	Random data	Mass data
Round robin	1622	2074	1298
On-demand	1306	1864	1000
FL prediction	1376	2021	1182

TABLE V. AVERAGE WAITING TIME PER BAG BEFORE (S)

Scenarios	Real data	Random data	Mass data
Round robin	41	57	14
On-demand	26	21	20
FL prediction	29	22	19

TABLE VI. IMPACT OF THE RECHARGING OF AIV BATTERIES

Scenarios	Number of recharges	Total duration of recharges	Total duration of simulation
Round robin	195	11760	3823
On-demand	622	9810	3683
FL prediction	198	11658	3793

Finally, we can discuss the benefits of using the communication capabilities of AIV agents. Indeed, adding communication between the AIVs and the infrastructure improves the performance of the Round Robin strategy (2% higher throughput and up to 11% fewer rounds for the AIVs). This communication also improves the results of the algorithm that determines whether an AIV needs to recharge. Indeed, by passing near the parking lot where the charging stations are located, the infrastructure can communicate to the AIV if one of the 4 stations is available. This information allows the AIVs to avoid waiting, especially to maintain a good level of baggage processing performance during periods of dense and continuous flow.

V. CONCLUSION AND PERSPECTIVES

In this article, we presented the context of fuzzy agent-based modelling and simulation. We introduced the general framework for modelling fuzzy agent-based applications, highlighting the fact that in such systems, each agent is responsible for its own knowledge and actions, which makes it an autonomous entity within the system.

It is important to note that the modelling of fuzzy agents is based on the fuzzy nature of knowledge, behaviours, and interactions.

We presented a case study involving the simulation of autonomous vehicle fleets for baggage handling in a simplified airport, in which each vehicle is simulated by a fuzzy agent. This simplification allows us to establish a baseline configuration to which we can add more complex and dynamic situations encountered in real airports, such as the introduction of baggage checkpoints requiring baggage drop-off and pick-up by the same or a different AIV.

We established a UML model of the automatic baggage handling system, providing both static and dynamic views of the circuit and the vehicles. Three different strategies were tested, with the goal of determining the number of AIVs that should circulate to handle the baggage arriving at the two entry points.

Finally, we presented our simulation results. These results allowed us to highlight the impact of various parameters, such as the number of simulations, the number of bags processed, the total simulation duration, and the total number of bags processed per hour.

We plan to continue improving the performance of fuzzy models in simulations of AIV agent behaviour for autonomous baggage handling in airports. This may consist of adding neural network-based learning capabilities [31][32], to increase the relevance and efficiency of their decisions in the collective management of their autonomies and in compliance with the performance expected by airport operators.

Another extension of our research consists of continuing work started recently, still in a simulation approach, on the incorporation of human-robot coworking aspects to maintain system performance, simulate the management of incidents occurring on the circuit or other types of problems difficult to solve for AIVs alone, and thus improve practical credibility for Airport 4.0 stakeholders.

ACKNOWLEDGMENT

The authors would like to thank the French Brittany region for funding the *ALPHA* project as part of the PME 2022 call for projects entitled "Accelerate time to market of digital technological innovations from SMEs in the Greater West."

REFERENCES

[1] A. G. Frank, L. S. Dalenogare, and N. F. Ayala, "Industry 4.0 technologies: Implementation patterns in manufacturing

companies," International journal of production economics, vol. 210, pp. 15-26, 2019.

[2] E. Oztemel and S. Gursev, "Literature review of Industry 4.0 and related technologies," Journal of intelligent manufacturing, vol. 31, no. 1, pp. 127-182, 2020.

[3] X. Xu, Y. Lu, B. Vogel-Heuser, and L. Wang, "Industry 4.0 and Industry 5.0—Inception, conception and perception," Journal of manufacturing systems, vol. 61, pp. 530-535, 2021.

[4] A. Akundi, et al., "State of Industry 5.0—Analysis and identification of current research trends," Applied System Innovation, vol. 5, no. 1, pp. 27, 2022.

[5] O. Oukacha, A.-J. Fougères, M. Djoko-Kouam, and E. Ostrosi, "Computational ergo-design for a real-time baggage handling system in an airport," Sustainability, vol. 17, no. 9, pp. 3794, 2025.

[6] N. Tsolakis, D. Bechtsis, and J.S. Srai, "Intelligent autonomous vehicles in digital supply chains: From conceptualisation, to simulation modelling, to real-world operations," Business Process Management Journal, vol. 25, no. 3, pp. 414-437, 2019.

[7] A. Hentout, M. Aouache, A. Maoudj, and I. Akli, "Human–robot interaction in industrial collaborative robotics: a literature review of the decade 2008–2017," Advanced Robotics, vol. 33, no. 15–16, pp. 764–799, 2019.

[8] R. Skapinyecz, "Examining the collision avoidance problem of AGVs in a discrete event simulation environment," Academic Journal of Manufacturing Engineering, vol. 22, no. 4, pp. 52-65, 2024.

[9] F. Gehlhoff, N. Jobs, and V. Henkel, "Agent-Based Control of Interaction Areas in Intralogistics: Concept, Implementation and Simulation," Logistics, vol. 9, no. 2, pp. 52, 2025.

[10] J. Huang, et al., "An overview of agent - based models for transport simulation and analysis," Journal of Advanced Transportation, vol. 2022, no. 1, pp. 1252534, 2022.

[11] J. Grosset, A.-J. Fougères, M. Djoko-Kouam, and J.-M. Bonnin, "Multi-agent Simulation of Autonomous Industrial Vehicle Fleets: Towards Dynamic Task Allocation in V2X Cooperation Mode," Integrated Computer-Aided Engineering, vol. 31, no. 3, pp. 249–266, 2024.

[12] P. Jing, H. Hu, F. Zhan, Y. Chen, and Y. Shi, "Agent-based simulation of autonomous vehicles: A systematic literature review," IEEE Access, vol. 8, pp. 79089-79103, 2020.

[13] A. Azadegan, L. Porobic, S. Ghazinoory, P. Samouei, and A. S. Kheirkhah, "Fuzzy logic in manufacturing: A review of literature and a specialized application," International Journal of Production Economics, vol. 132, no. 2, pp. 258-270, 2011.

[14] H. H. Tang and N. S. Ahmad, "Fuzzy logic approach for controlling uncertain and nonlinear systems: a comprehensive review of applications and advances," Systems Science & Control Engineering, vol. 12, no. 1, pp. 2394429, 2024.

[15] L. A. Zadeh, "Fuzzy sets. Information and control, vol. 8, no. 3, pp. 338-353, 1965.

[16] L. A. Zadeh, "Outline of a new approach to the analysis of complex systems and decision processes," IEEE Transactions on systems, Man, and Cybernetics, vol. 3, no. 1, pp. 28-44, 1973.

[17] N. Ghasem-Aghaee and T.I. Ören, "Towards Fuzzy Agents with Dynamic Personality for Human Behavior Simulation," in Proc. of SCSC 2003, Montreal, Canada, 2003, pp. 3–10.

[18] A.-J. Fougères, "A Modelling Approach Based on Fuzzy Agent," Int. J. of Computer Science Issues, vol. 9, no. 6, pp. 19-28, 2013.

[19] A. Meylani, et al., "Different Types of Fuzzy Logic in Obstacles Avoidance of Mobile Robot," Int. Conf. on Electrical. Eng. and Computer Sc., 2018, pp. 93-100.

[20] B.K. Patle, et al., "A review: On path planning strategies for navigation of mobile robot," Defence Technology, vol. 15, no. 4, pp. 582-606, 2019.

[21] M. Alakhras, M. Oussalah, and M. Hussein, "A survey of fuzzy logic in wireless localization," EURASIP J. on Wireless Com. and Networking, vol. 1, pp. 1-45, 2020.

[22] M.F.R. Lee and A. Nugroho, "Intelligent Energy Management System for Mobile Robot," Sustainability, vol. 14, no. 16, pp. 10056, 2022.

[23] P. K. Biswas, "Towards an agent-oriented approach to conceptualization," Applied Soft Computing, vol. 8, no. 1, pp. 127-139, 2008.

[24] B. Bauer and J. Odell, "UML 2.0 and agents: how to build agent-based systems with the new UML standard," Engineering Applications of Artificial Intelligence, vol. 18, pp. 141–157, 2005.

[25] A.-J. Fougères, "Agents to cooperate in distributed design," in the IEEE International Conference on Systems, Man and Cybernetics, (SMC'04), The Hague, Netherlands, October 10-13, 2004, vol. 3, pp. 2629-2634.

[26] E. Ostrosi, A.-J. Fougères, and M. Ferney, "Fuzzy Agents for Product Configuration in Collaborative and Distributed Design Process," Applied Soft Computing, vol. 8, no. 12, pp. 2091–2105, 2012.

[27] A.-J. Fougères and E. Ostrosi, "Holonic Fuzzy Agents for Integrated CAD Product and Adaptive Manufacturing Cell Formation," Journal of Integrated Design and Process Science, vol. 23, no. 1, pp. 77-102, 2019.

[28] A.-J. Fougères and E. Ostrosi, "Multiple Fuzzy Roles: Analysis of their Evolving in a Fuzzy Agent-Based Collaborative Design Platform," In: Lecture Notes Studies in Computational Intelligence (LNCSI), Edited by K. Madani, A. Dourado, A. Rosa, J. Filipe and J. Kacprzyk, Springer International Publishing Switzerland, 2016, p.207-226, ISBN: 978-3-319-23391-8, 978-3-319-23392-5 (e-book).

[29] A.-J. Fougères and E. Ostrosi, "Fuzzy engineering design semantics elaboration and application," Soft Computing Letters, vol. 3, pp. 100025, 2021.

[30] J. Grosset, A.-J. Fougères, M. Djoko-Kouam, and J.-M. Bonnin, "Fuzzy Agent-Based Simulations of Cooperative Strategies for Task Allocation, Collision Avoidance, and Battery Charging Management of Autonomous Industrial Vehicles," International Journal on Advances in Systems and Measurements, vol. 18, no. 1&2, pp. 8-18, 2025.

[31] D. Luviano-Cruz, et al., "Multi-agent reinforcement learning using linear fuzzy model applied to cooperative mobile robots," Symmetry, vol. 10, no. 10, pp. 461., 2018

[32] H.M. Yudha, T. Dewi, and N. Hasana, "Performance comparison of fuzzy logic and neural network design for mobile robot navigation," Int. Conf. on Electrical Eng. and Comp. Sc., 2019, pp. 79-84, 2019.

VR-ANN: Visualization of Artificial Neural Network Models in Virtual Reality

Roy Oberhauser[0000-0002-7606-8226]
Computer Science Dept.
Aalen University
Aalen, Germany
e-mail: roy.oberhauser@hs-aalen.de

Abstract – **Artificial Neural Networks (ANNs or NNs) are used in Deep Learning (DL), a subset of Machine Learning (ML). And yet, especially to novices or infrequent users, ANNs can seem abstract and mathematical, and not readily accessible and understandable. Furthermore, a model's configuration and output results may not be comprehensible and obvious. To make ANN models more accessible and support comprehension and analysis even for large models, this paper contributes our VR-ANN solution concept for immersive ANN visualization in Virtual Reality (VR). Its feasibility is demonstrated with a prototype, while a case-based evaluation provides insights into its capabilities and potential for supporting ANN model building, comprehension, analysis, and collaboration.**

Keywords – artificial neural networks; visualization; virtual reality; deep learning; machine learning.

I. Introduction

Machine Learning (ML) is a subset of Artificial Intelligence (AI) that focuses on having machines learn from data, improving their performance over time without reprogramming [1]. A learning algorithm can optimize its model's parameters to improve its performance, which can improve pattern detection, predictions, decisions, etc. Various models can be applied in the area of ML. Artificial NNs (ANNs), referred to as just Neural Networks (NNs) in this paper, are inspired by biological NNs and consist of nodes (referred to as artificial neurons) connected via weighted links or edges (i.e., synapses), with other nodes and are aggregated into layers. Numbers are used to represent signals, while a node's activation function determines a neuron's output based on its inputs and their associated link weights. Between the input and output layer are intermediate (hidden) layers. Dense layers are fully-connected to the preceding layer. Dropout layers address overfitting by randomly setting a fraction of the input units to that layer to 0 during training. Hidden layers are any that are neither input nor output layers. Deep Learning (DL) is a branch of ML utilizing deep NNs having multiple hidden layers. Convolutional Neural Networks (CNNs) are a type of DL network especially relevant for image processing. Feedforward NNs (FNNs) are a type of NN where all neurons are fully connected to the next layer with unidirectional information flow. Recurrent NNs (RNNs) are a type of NN for processing sequential data where its order matters.

Visualization of NN models can support comprehension, analysis, and learning, and while various tools support 2D, there has been relatively little investigation into the potential offered by Virtual Reality (VR). To address a comprehensive visualization of NN models, this paper proposes and investigates an immersive VR experience. In prior work, we investigated the application of VR to various other areas. A selection of our prior VR-related contributions include: in the Software Engineering (SE) space, VR-SDLC [2] models development lifecycles, VR-Git [3] models Git repositories, VR-DevOps [4] models Continuous Development pipelines, VR-SBOM [5] models Software Bill of Materials (SBOM) and software supply chains, and VR-EA+TCK [6] and VR-EvoEA+BP [7] exemplify enterprise modeling and business processes. This paper contributes a solution concept towards immersive visualization of ANNs in VR. A prototype demonstrates its feasibility, while a case-based evaluation provides insights into its capabilities and potential for supporting ANN model building, comprehension, analysis, and collaboration.

The structure of this paper is as follows: the next section discusses related work. Section 3 describes our solution. Section 4 presents our realization and is followed by our evaluation in Section 5. And finally, a conclusion is provided.

II. Related Work

In their survey of the application of XR to AI, Hirzle et al. [8] screened 2619 publications (2017-2021) and reviewed 311 in depth. They found only seven papers that applied XR to AI problems (2.3%), five of which visualize AI methods for immersive analytics, or to improve the understanding of neural networks for non-expert users by visualizing them in VR (the rest are discussed below). The authors state XR "methods are promising to facilitate the interaction with neural networks for novices." The 2025 survey by Yim and Su [9] of K-12 learning tools for AI examined 46 papers, but and makes no mention any XR/VR tool. The 2021 survey by Reiners et al. [10] identified 36 papers that combined XR and AI, of which only two were non-domain-specific and related to visualizing DL in XR (discussed below). The survey on AI in VR by Inkarbekov et al. [11] identified a research gap for more user-friendly, intuitive, and adaptable VR tools that can accommodate complex and high-dimensional AI models. From these surveys we conclude that VR-based visualization of AI has not been thoroughly investigated nor readily adopted and remains relatively unexplored.

VR-related NN visualization work includes Bellgardt et al. [12], who depict convolutional ANNs in VR as node-link diagrams by stacking circular layers for a robotic image processing case. InteractML [13] is a node-based tool for creative practitioners to train an ML model for movement interactions in VR using real-time gesture demonstrations. AIive [14] uses a force-directed graph visualization and sonification to enable VR users to manipulate NN parameters via virtual hands and auditory feedback. Towards non-experts, Meissler et al. [15][16] depict a simplified CNN model in 3D in a closed room virtual environment, with information in 2D anchored to different areas of the room. Schreiber and Bock [17] use the Unreal Engine to display a NN in 3D, whereby connections between layers are not visualized. While VR is mentioned in the title, there is no mention of VR or immersion in the paper, which focuses on 3D. Queck et al. [18] create a virtual room in VR with areas providing CNN information. VR4DL [19] can train and test CNNs with a focus on biomedical image classification; it is not intended to be generic for arbitrary CNNs, and is tailored to users with little to no knowledge of ML. DeepVisionVR [20] visualizes CNNs in VR with a focus on image processing.

Common 2D NN model visualization tools include (TensorFlow) Deep playground, TensorBoard, Netron, Comet, and neptune.ai.

III. Solution Concept

Our VR-ANN solution concept is shown (in blue) in the ML area relative to our other prior VR solutions in our conceptual map of Figure 1. Our generalized VR Modeling Framework (VR-MF) (detailed in [21]) is the foundation, which provides a domain-independent hypermodeling framework, which addresses the VR aspects of visualization, navigation, interaction, and data integration. Our VR-based solutions specific to the Enterprise Architecture (EA) and Business Process (BP) space (EA & BP) include: VR-EA [21] for mapping EA models to VR, VR-BPMN [22] for BPMN models, VR-EAT for enterprise repository integration, VR-EA+TCK [6] for knowledge and content integration, and VR-EvoEA+BP [7] for EA evolution and business process animation, VR-ProcessMine, and VR-SBOM [5]. Solutions in the SE and Systems Engineering (SysE) areas include: VR-Git [3], VR-GitCity, and VR-GitEvo+CI/CD for git-related solutions, VR-DevOps [4], VR-V&V (Verification and Validation), VR-TestCoverage, VR-SDLC [2], VR-ISA for informed software architectures, and VR-UML and VR-SysML for software and systems modeling.

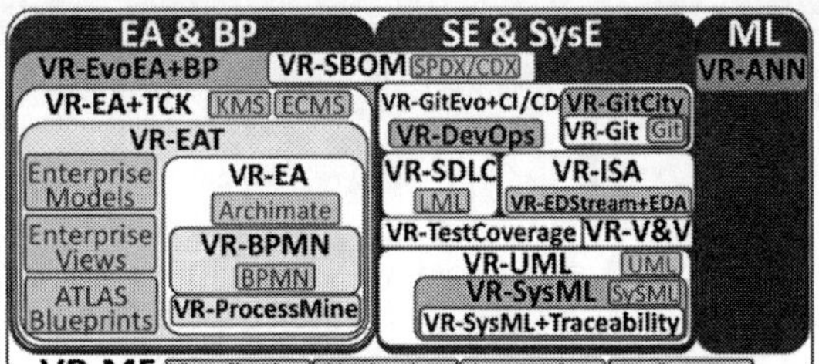

Figure 1. Conceptual map of our various published VR solution concepts with VR-ANN highlighted in blue.

A. Visualization in VR

To better delimit the context of a NN model in a multi-NN VR space, each NN model is visualized within an outlined 3D transparent Boundary Box (BB) placed on a *hyperplane*. This enables further additional portfolio of NNs to be visualized contemporaneously. Contained within the NN BB are outlined transparent 3D BBs, each representing a NN layer, which vertically delineates a set of spherical nodes (neurons). Lines are used as connectors to indicate which nodes are connected between layers.

B. Navigation in VR

Dual navigation modes are incorporated in our solution: default gliding controls for fly-through VR, while teleporting instantly places the camera at a selected position in space. While teleporting can be potentially disconcerting, it may reduce the likelihood of VR sickness.

C. Interaction in VR

User-element interaction is supported primarily through VR controllers and the incorporation of a VR-Tablet. The VR-Tablet provides detailed context-specific element information. Various tabs in the VR-Tablet enable support for loading, training, executing, or configuring NN models and viewing related graphs. Since for our examples no text entry and keyboard were required, a virtual keyboard was not included. However, our implementation can be readily enhanced with a virtual keyboard for text entry using laser pointer key selection, as demonstrated in our other VR solutions. A small control sphere is placed as an affordance at the bottom front corner on the boundary of the hyperplane for dragging, collapsing (to reduce visual clutter), or expanding a NN BB.

IV. Realization

For our prototype realization, the VR visualization aspects were implemented using Unity in C#, referred to as our frontend, as shown in Figure 2. It connects via a Socket to our backend Data Hub, which is based on the hexagonal (or ports-and-adapters) design pattern and is implemented in Python. It integrates and stores all data via PyMongo to a MongoDB database in JSON/BSON format.

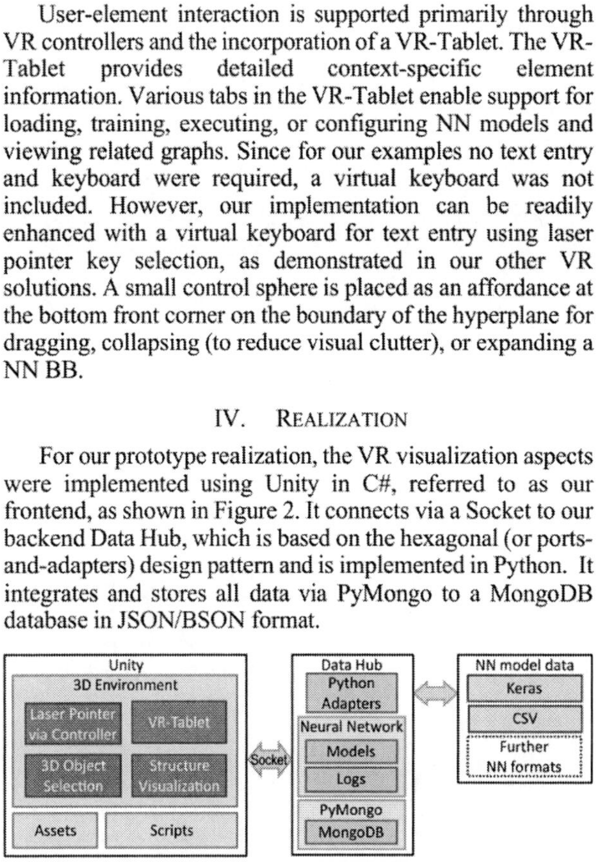

Figure 2. VR-ANN logical architecture.

NN model support is implemented within the Data Hub in Python. The Keras API was used as a high-level DL API primarily due to its popularity and flexibility, since it supports multiple backends, such as TensorFlow, PyTorch, OpenVINO, and JAX (Python library for high-performance ML). Initially for prototyping, the Sequential model with various layer types placed in sequence is supported, but support for additional models can be readily added.

Data can be imported from or exported to the common keras format (.keras extension), which is a zip archive containing JSON-based configuration, H5-based state file containing layers and weights, model weights, and metadata. Additionally, the CSV file format is supported. Further formats can be readily supported via adapters. The models can either be pretrained, loaded, and executed in VR (load and execute), or can be (re)configured and trained in a VR session via our Model Builder support mode.

To exemplify the internal interaction, a sequence diagram for a VR-centric training session is shown in Figure 3. Initially, the list of available NN projects is retrieved from the Data Hub. If the user creates a new model and starts a training session, then the layer data is sent to the Data Hub, the training inputs are retrieved, and a model is created and trained via the Keras API, training values are logged, and the model is saved or exported. The acquired layer data is returned to Unity via the socket, and is visualized as a model, which can be further analyzed.

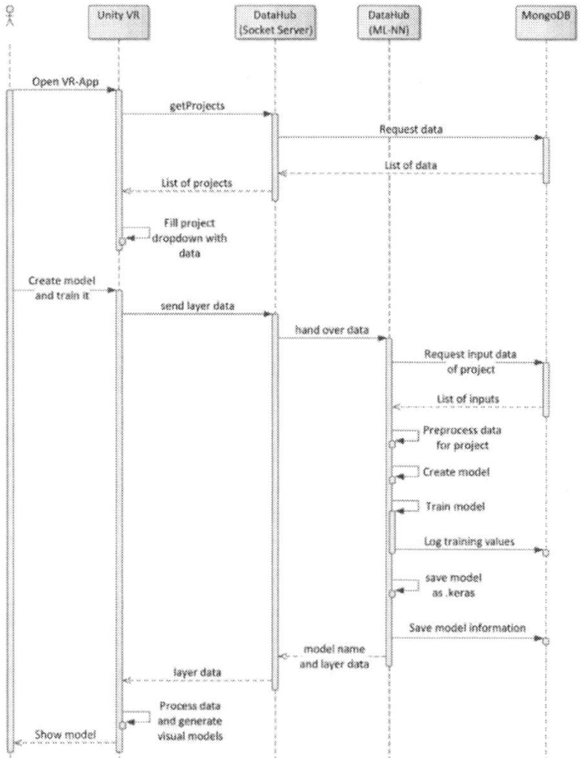

Figure 3. VR-ANN sequence diagram for a VR-centric training session.

To support VR interaction, we implemented the VR-Tablet as shown in the bottom right in Figure 4. The tab groups Load, Training, Execution, Display options, and Graphs are shown, as is the scrollbar. Here, under the selected Display options tab, the epoch slider is shown as well as options to show or color connections. Also shown in this figure, the model layer BBs top side provide layer information (number and type) and metrics (number of neurons) and containing spheres as neurons evenly spaced along a single vertical plane with slots for the next best-fitting square matrix, filled from the bottom left (upper right may have empty slots), while dropout layers are depicted as an opaque slab. Connectors are shown by default in blue; the diameter of the lines indicate the relative weighting to the next layer.

In execution, the most active (top five) routes as nodes and connectors are colored (darker to lighter) green. Connectors can optionally be colored (iterated list of 32 colors) to more easily follow a connector between nodes.

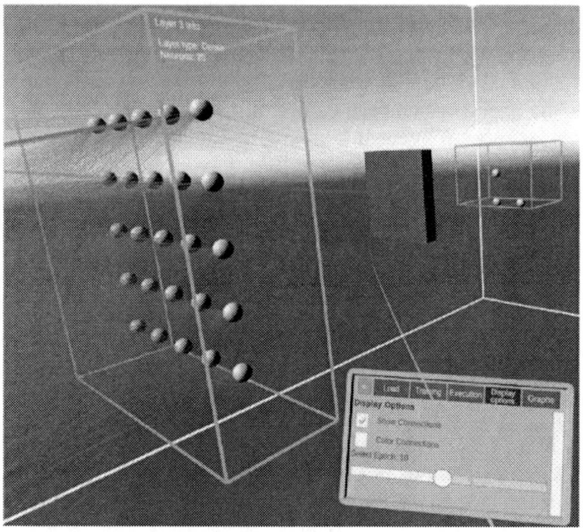

Figure 4. BBs and VR-Tablet showing tab groups and input options.

To support Model Builder mode, opaque 3D boxes represent layers ordered from left to right, each of which offers appropriate options based on type, as shown in Figure 5. To avoid requiring text input and simplify interaction, the default values can be adjusted with plus/minus buttons and dropdown lists offer selection options. Layers can be removed by an X button at the top right, and new layer types can be inserted via the VR-Tablet. The ordering of the layers can be adjusted by dragging the boxes. RNN support was not yet implemented. All applicable parameters can be selected in the VR-Tablet, including epochs, learning rate, optimizer, loss function, etc.

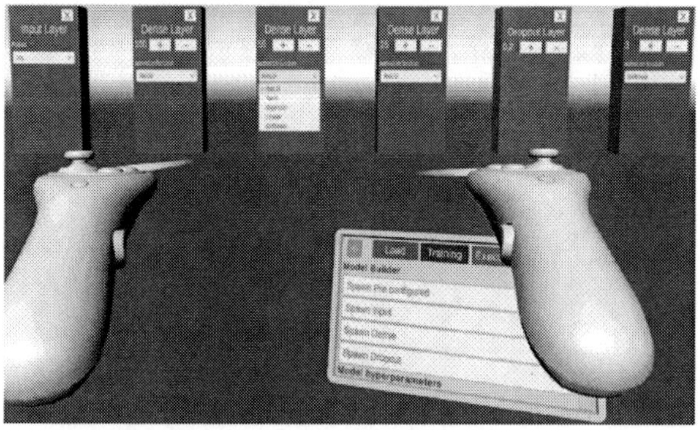

Figure 5. Model Builder for defining and configuring a NN.

Support for spawning two graph types was implemented: a loss graph and an accuracy graph, each of which also offer a corner sphere affordance for flexible placement or collapsing.

V. Evaluation

The evaluation of our VR-ANN solution concept is based on the design science method and principles [24], in particular a viable artifact, problem relevance, and design evaluation (utility, quality, efficacy). A case study is used based on the following scenarios: comparison to 2D visualization, build and train support, analysis support, and scaling support.

A. 2D vs. VR-ANN Visualization

To visually compare a typical NN tool's 2D visual representation of a NN to VR-ANN, an FNN is shown in the TensorFlow Playground in Figure 6. The equivalent NN in VR-ANN is shown in Figure 7. The VR-ANN model is immersively accessible, and can be readily investigated and analyzed. Much of the information seen in the 2D playground is available in VR by interacting with the VR-Tablet or elements (layer, nodes). Given many connections in 2D, we contend it to be more straightforward to immersively follow a connector in VR separated spatially in 3D space.

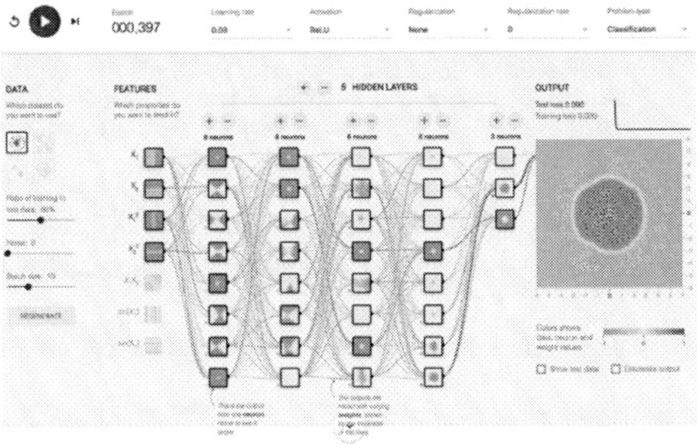

Figure 6. Screenshot of a NN model in TensorFlow playground [25].

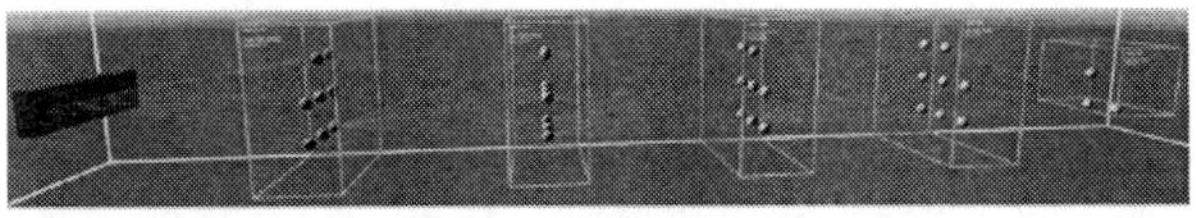

Figure 7. Equivalent NN in VR-ANN containing layers as BBs of connected nodes.

B. Build and Train NN Model Support

Support for building NNs was shown in Figure 5. Via the VR-Tablet, a preconfigured existing model can be loaded, or additional layer types flexibly. Once trained, the model

C. Analysis Support

To demonstrate analysis support, we utilize an Iris flower dataset available on Kaggle [26]. For this, 50 samples each of three Iris species (Setosa, Versicolor, Virginica) are classified in the output based on four properties: SepalLengthCm, SepalWidthCm, PetalLengthCm, PetalWidthCm. After building and training, the entire model with all layer types and neurons is visualized within a BB as was shown in Figure 7. This helps in comprehension of the total number of layers and their type, size, and ordering. Metrics are provided on each layer BB as seen in the upper right of Figure 8. As shown, the connections between neurons can be optionally colored to help differentiate them when immersively following a connection.

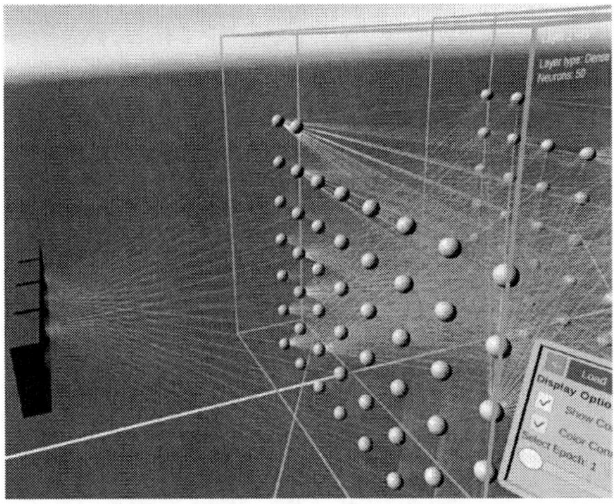

Figure 8. Colored connections between neurons.

To support more detailed analysis, selecting a single node will cause only connections related to that node to be shown and all others to be hidden, as seen in Figure 9. Here, the weight values of all the connected input nodes are displayed above each input node in the previous layer, metadata about the selected node is shown in a panel above that node, such as bias and output values, and output connections are visible.

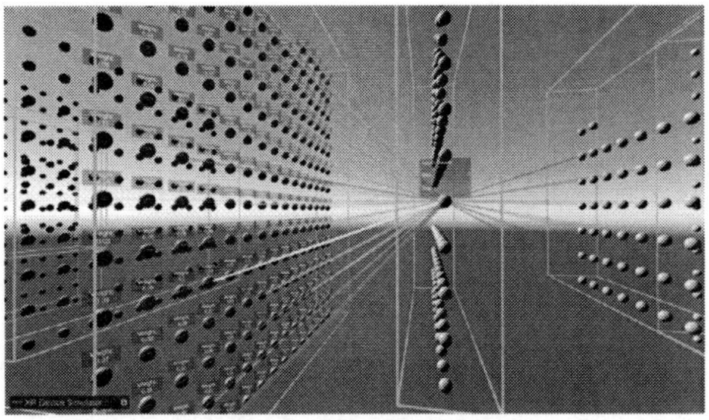

Figure 9. Node selection shows details related to that node.

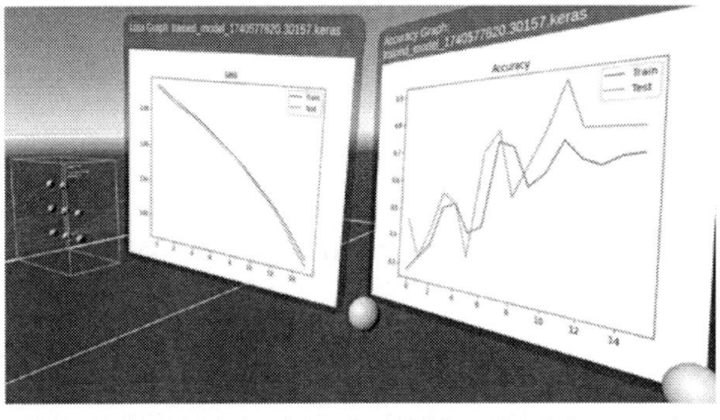

Figure 10. Loss (center) and Accuracy (right) graphs relative to epochs.

Beyond the data available in the VR-Tablet, rather than just have the graphs in the VR-Tablet, a loss graph and/or accuracy graph can be spawned (and moved or collapsed via the affordances) and retained with the model context as shown in Figure 10. Thus, when multiple similar models or slightly different configurations are loaded in VR, one can more readily determine the differences.

The inputs can be adjusted as shown in Figure 11 (left), and via the VR-Tablet the model executed. The top classification result for this data set can be seen in Figure 11 (right). After NN execution, the top five most frequent activation paths (pathways, routes) are indicated via (darker-to-lighter) green nodes and connectors as shown in Figure 12.

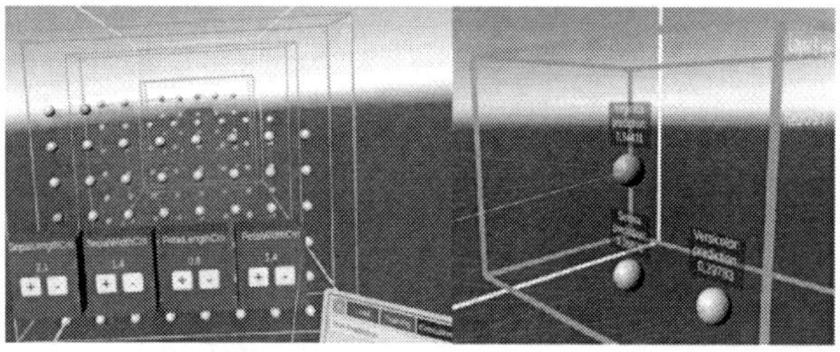

Figure 11. Execution on inputs (left) and result in the output layer (right).

Figure 12. Overall top primary active routes (green nodes and connectors).

D. Scaling Support

To demonstrate the scaling ability of VR to support large NN models, Figure 13 depicts a mid-sized model that consists of ten (8 hidden) layers with 432 neurons counts (4, 100, 50, 25, 100, 50, 25, 50, 25, dropout, 3). Figure 14 shows a large model consisting of 982 neurons across ten (8 hidden) layers (4, 100, 200, 25, 100, 200, 100, 50, 200, 3) with the connectors colored. Our principle is to initially depict a model's reality with its inherent complexity. However, as shown in the analysis case, via immersion, selection of an element of interest, display filtering such as turning off connectors, visual overload can be addressed. Based on the stakeholder's interest and intentionality, comprehension or issue analysis for large models can be supported and stakeholder collaboration opportunities with a common immersive model utilized.

VI. Conclusion

This paper described our VR-ANN contribution, a solution concept towards immersive visualization of ANNs in VR. Our prototype demonstrates its feasibility. The case-based evaluation provides insights into its capabilities and potential for immersively supporting the comprehension, building, configuring, training, and analysis of ANN models and related stakeholder collaboration. The scaling case showcased its ability to immersively depict large models, which could benefit more advanced users when the models become much larger than what current 2D models can readily display, or when investigating anomalies or issues. Future work includes RNN and CNN support, additional framework and format support, and a comprehensive empirical study.

Acknowledgment

The author would like to thank Daniel Godeck for his assistance with the design, implementation, and screenshots.

References

[1] S. Russell and P. Norvig, Artificial Intelligence: A Modern Approach, Global Edition, 4th ed. Pearson Education, 2021. ISBN 978-0-1346-1099-3.

[2] R. Oberhauser, "VR-SDLC: A Context-Enhanced Life Cycle Visualization of Software-or-Systems Development in Virtual Reality," In: Business Modeling and Software Design (BMSD 2024), LNBIP, vol 523, Springer, Cham, 2024, pp. 112-129, https://doi.org/10.1007/978-3-031-64073-5_8.

[3] R. Oberhauser, "VR-Git: Git Repository Visualization and Immersion in Virtual Reality," 17th Int'l Conf. on Software Engineering Advances (ICSEA 2022), IARIA, 2022, pp. 9-14.

[4] R. Oberhauser, "VR-DevOps: Visualizing and Interacting with DevOps Pipelines in Virtual Reality," Nineteenth International Conference on Software Engineering Advances (ICSEA 2024), IARIA, 2024, pp. 43-48.

[5] R. Oberhauser, "VR-SBOM: Visualization of Software Bill of Materials and Software Supply Chains in Virtual Reality," In: Business Modeling and Software Design (BMSD 2025), LNBIP, vol 559, Springer, Cham, 2025, pp. 52-70, https://doi.org/10.1007/978-3-031-98033-6_4.

[6] R. Oberhauser, M. Baehre, and P. Sousa, "VR-EA+TCK: Visualizing Enterprise Architecture, Content, and Knowledge in Virtual Reality," In: Business Modeling and Software Design (BMSD 2022), LNBIP, vol 453, Springer, 2022, pp. 122-140. https://doi.org/10.1007/978-3-031-11510-3_8.

[7] R. Oberhauser, M. Baehre, and P. Sousa, "VR-EvoEA+BP: Using Virtual Reality to Visualize Enterprise Context Dynamics Related to Enterprise Evolution and Business Processes," In: Business Modeling and Software Design (BMSD 2023), LNBIP, vol 483, Springer, 2023, pp. 110-128, https://doi.org/10.1007/978-3-031-36757-1_7.

[8] T. Hirzle et al., "When XR and AI Meet - A Scoping Review on Extended Reality and Artificial Intelligence," In: Proceedings of the 2023 CHI Conference on Human Factors in Computing Systems (CHI '23), ACM, Article 730, 2023, pp. 1–45. https://doi.org/10.1145/3544548.3581072.

[9] I. Yim and J. Su, "Artificial intelligence (AI) learning tools in K-12 education: A scoping review," Journal on Computers in Education, Vol. 12, pp. 93–131, 2025, https://doi.org/10.1007/s40692-023-00304-9.

[10] D. Reiners, M. R. Davahli, W. Karwowski, and C. Cruz-Neira, "The combination of artificial intelligence and extended reality: A systematic review," Frontiers in Virtual Reality, 2, 721933, 2021, doi: 10.3389/frvir.2021.721933

[11] M. Inkarbekov, R. Monahan, and B. A. Pearlmutter, "Visualization of ai systems in virtual reality: A comprehensive review," arXiv preprint, 2023, arXiv:2306.15545.

[12] M. Bellgardt, C. Scheiderer and T. W. Kuhlen, "An Immersive Node-Link Visualization of Artificial Neural Networks for Machine Learning Experts," 2020 IEEE International Conf. on Artificial Intelligence and Virtual Reality (AIVR), IEEE, 2020, pp. 33-36, doi: 10.1109/AIVR50618.2020.00015.

[13] C. Hilton et al., "InteractML: Making machine learning accessible for creative practitioners working with movement interaction in immersive media," In: Proceedings of the 27th ACM Symposium on Virtual Reality Software and Technology (VRST '21), ACM, Article 23, 2021, pp. 1–10. https://doi.org/10.1145/3489849.3489879.

[14] Z. Lyu, J. Li and B. Wang, "AIive: Interactive Visualization and Sonification of Neural Networks in Virtual Reality," 2021 IEEE International Conference on Artificial Intelligence and Virtual Reality (AIVR), IEEE, 2021, pp. 251-255, doi: 10.1109/AIVR52153.2021.00057.

[15] N. Meissler, A. Wohlan, N. Hochgeschwender, and A. Schreiber, "Using Visualization of Convolutional Neural Networks in Virtual Reality for Machine Learning Newcomers," 2019 IEEE International Conference on Artificial Intelligence and Virtual Reality (AIVR), IEEE, 2019, pp. 152-1526, doi: 10.1109/AIVR46125.2019.00031.

[16] A. Wohlan, N. Hochgeschwender, and N. Meissler, "Visualizing Convolutional Neural Networks with Virtual Reality," In: Proc. 25th ACM Symposium on Virtual Reality Software and Technology (VRST '19). ACM, Article 100, pp. 1–2, 2019, https://doi.org/10.1145/3359996.3364817

[17] A. Schreiber and M. Bock, "Visualization and exploration of deep learning networks in 3D and virtual reality," In: Human-Computer Interaction International 2019 (HCII 2019) Posters, Proc. 21st International Conference on HCI (HCII 2019), CCIS, Springer International Publishing, 2019, pp. 206-211.

[18] D. Queck, A. Wohlan, and A. Schreiber, „Neural Network Visualization in Virtual Reality: A Use Case Analysis and Implementation," In: Human Interface and the Management of Information: Visual and Information Design (HCII 2022), LNCS, Springer, 2022, vol 13305, pp. 384-397, https://doi.org/10.1007/978-3-031-06424-1_28.

[19] K. VanHorn and M. C. Çobanoğlu, "Democratizing AI in biomedical image classification using virtual reality," Virtual Reality, 26(1), pp. 159-171, 2021, https://doi.org/10.1007/s10055-021-00550-1

[20] C. Linse, A. Hammam, and T. Martinetz, "A walk in the black-box: 3D visualization of large neural networks in virtual reality," Neural Computing and Applications, vol. 34, no. 23, pp. 21237-21252, 2022.

[21] R. Oberhauser and C. Pogolski, "VR-EA: Virtual Reality Visualization of Enterprise Architecture Models with ArchiMate and BPMN," In: Business Modeling and Software Design (BMSD 2019), LNBIP, vol. 356, Springer, Cham, 2019, pp. 170-187, https://doi.org/10.1007/978-3-030-24854-3_11.

[22] R. Oberhauser, C. Pogolski, and A. Matic, "VR-BPMN: Visualizing BPMN models in Virtual Reality," In: Shishkov, B. (ed.) Business Modeling and Software Design (BMSD 2018), LNBIP, vol. 319, Springer, 2018, pp. 83–97, https://doi.org/10.1007/978-3-319-94214-8_6.

[23] R. Oberhauser, "VR-GitCity: Immersively Visualizing Git Repository Evolution Using a City Metaphor in Virtual Reality," International Journal on Advances in Software, 16 (3 & 4), 2023, pp. 141-150.

[24] A.R. Hevner, S.T. March, J. Park, and S. Ram, "Design science in information systems research," MIS Quarterly, 28(1), 2004, pp. 75-105.

[25] [Online]. Available from: https://playground.tensorflow.org 2025.08.01

[26] [Online]. Available from: https://www.kaggle.com/code/ranjeetjain3/visualization-machine-learning-deep-learning 2025.08.01

Figure 13. Mid-sized model consisting of 8 hidden layers and 432 neurons.

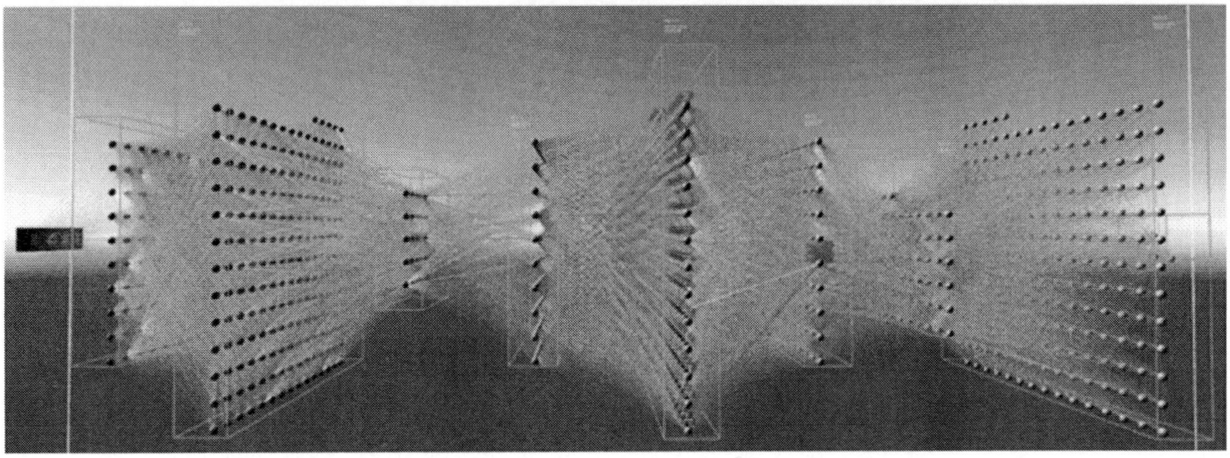

Figure 14. Large model (8 hidden layers and 982 neurons) with colored connections.